Virgin and Whore

For Allan

Virgin and Whore

*The Image of Women
in the Poetry
of William Carlos Williams*

by
Audrey T. Rodgers

McFarland & Company, Inc., Publishers
Jefferson, North Carolina, and London

Acknowledgments

I welcome this opportunity to thank friends and colleagues who have offered me their insights, encouragement, and good wishes during the writing of this book. I am especially appreciative of the suggestions made by Mr. John Pickering of the Pennsylvania State University Press after his careful reading of the manuscript, for the enthusiastic support of Evelyn Hinz, editor of *Mosaic*, and for the quiet confidence and help of Professor Peter White of the University of New Mexico.

A special thanks must go to Mr. James Laughlin, whose reminiscences of William Carlos Williams and whose precious store of Williams' letters gave a special kind of life to this study.

I owe a debt of gratitude to the Institute for Arts & Humanistic Studies, directed by Professor Stanley Weintraub, for research aid and to the Pennsylvania State University Liberal Arts Faculty Research Fund for several grants-in-aid.

Finally, I thank my husband, Dr. Allan Rodgers who, as a geographer, thinks spatially and gave me "a room of one's own" to make this project come to fruition.

Library of Congress Cataloguing-in-Publication Data

Rodgers, Audrey T.
  Virgin and whore.

  Bibliography: p. 165.
  Includes index.
  1. Williams, William Carlos, 1883–1963 — Criticism and interpretation.   2. Women in literature.   I. Title.
PS3545.I544Z875   1987   811'.52   86-43083

ISBN 0-89950-279-2 (acid-free natural paper)

Printed in the United States of America.

McFarland   Box 611   Jefferson NC 28640

Contents

—the virgin and the whore, which
most endures? the world
of the imagination most endures:

Paterson V

Introduction

Most poets live in several worlds: William Carlos Williams was surely no exception. Wallace Stevens worked for the Hartford Accident and Indemnity Company; T.S. Eliot worked for Lloyd's Bank before he became editor of the *Criterion*; Frost labored on five farms over a long period of his "life in the clearing." Few poets—Hart Crane, Ezra Pound, and the poets in the academy: Roethke, Hoffman, Eberhart, and Penn Warren among others—enjoyed the luxury of retreating to the solitary writing of poetry far from the distractions of workaday life. Denise Levertov and May Sarton have made painfully clear how difficult that stolen time was to capture. Among the poets who worked in the "real" world, there was always a distancing from the world of the creative imagination.

Yet William Carlos Williams led an active and fruitful life as a full-time physician and full-time poet. He was very much aware that the juxtaposition of these worlds, while often in conflict, generated a body of poetry that emphasized "experience" as the only valid subject matter for poetry. "No ideas but in things," sought to establish the rule that the poetic imagination draws from palpable fact the raw material of the poem. The poem then fuses Williams' twin worlds: the bustling inchoate world of Rutherford, New Jersey, and the world of the creative imagination, a mélange of the personal past, memory, history itself.

On one level, the subject of this book is the image of woman in the poetry of William Carlos Williams. No sustained study of this central image in Williams' work has been made. The title "The Virgin and the Whore," coming directly from Book Five of *Paterson*, suggests a more complex goal of this study, one noted only in passing by most Williams scholars; namely, the development of the image of the virgin/whore as it relates to the poet's own notion of the artistic process. For Williams, the virgin frequently became associated with the pure, white-hot flame of the imagination, always in danger of violation. Sometimes he called it the "radiant gist"—that purity that Madame Curie revealed in the common pitchblende. The whore, as I hope to demonstrate, is experience, revealed in the prosaic, often vulgar world teeming with life. The importance of the virgin and the whore, while not explicitly termed until the advent of *Paterson*, had its beginnings in the seminal

1

poem "The Wanderer." The river spirit, the hag, exhorts the young innocent to leap into the filthy Passaic, where he will discover life and art.

The process of this study is thus to measure the degree to which a singular facet of Williams' "real" world contributed to one aspect of his art: the image of the virgin/whore as a counterpart for his own artistic experience. "I am Kora,"* he often proclaimed. As a physician, by his own admission, he aided in the birth of 2000 babies! He worked in hospitals surrounded by nurses; he visited sick children and women who had suffered violation. Confessing that he "almost puked" at the filth, tragedy, and ugliness in the struggle of miserable lives, he nevertheless made them part of his art. Though Rutherford was by and large a middle-class community and Williams attended it, he drew his subject matter for poetry from the victims of that urban society that had exploited, or ignored, or corrupted the unenlightened masses.

In addition, I hope to establish the idea that Williams' complex and original view of women grew as well from his fascination with two myths: the violation of Kore/Persephone and the seduction of the unicorn by the virgin/whore, depicted in the French tapestries hanging on the walls of the Cloisters across the Hudson. I hope to demonstrate that Williams' view of the "female principle" became a hallmark of his poetry, unique in the poetry of the twentieth century. I would emphasize his belief, often articulated in prose and poetry, that man is incomplete without woman. Fundamental to this view was Williams' acceptance, as expressed by Reed Whittemore (*William Carlos Williams: Poet from New Jersey* [New York: Houghton Mifflin, 1975, p. 198]), that "the male in isolation from the female was abstract and impractical, was a rootless tumbling weed, and hence needed constantly the female presence. . . ." I shall probe the significance of that view as it shaped the poetry, necessitating a *rapid* look at the actual women in Williams' life. This would in no way repeat the autobiographical matter dealt with in Paul Mariani's exhaustive study, *William Carlos Williams: A New World Naked.* Williams scholarship, and this study in particular, is most indebted to Mariani, whose examination of the many facets of Williams' long career as poet and doctor confirms much that is hinted in the poetry and prose. Where disagreements arise between Mariani's evaluation of the impact of Williams' grandmother and mother on the poet and Williams' own perceptions, I have tended to accept Williams' own view of their influence, since the poetic models for these women and others emerge from his recollections, inexact as they may have been!

The first chapter briefly traces the history of the virgin and the whore and compares and contrasts it with Williams' own definition. However,

---

*Greek myth refers to either "Kore" or "Core"; Williams' consistent use of "Kora" may have come from Pound, or simply his preference for a more pronounced emphasis the spelling would provide for poetic rhythm.

when Williams uses the image of the oxymoron *explicitly* in *Paterson*, I have reserved a definition of that figure where it is most applicable.

Chapter II examines the myth of Kore/Demeter that manifested the "female principle." Although I have emphasized those sources in mythology familiar to Williams, it should be noted that the more recent scholarship of mythographers like George Mylonas, G.S. Kirk, and Paul Friedrich (postdating the majority of Williams' work) put into question many of Frazer's and Graves' basic interpretations of traditional myths. If Frazer was incorrect in designating Demeter and Aphrodite as vegetation gods, Williams chose to see them as such, accommodating his own view of the female principle. In addition, it should be noted that when such studies as those by Jung and Kerenyi enlarge and enhance Williams' own notions of androgyny, I have chosen to indicate them. In this way, we may still appreciate Williams' approach to myths and archetypes that were popularized in his time, while realizing that those theories have become newly interpreted by reputable mythographers and psychologists.

Chapter III, briefly biographical, touches upon the important women in the poet's life as juxtapositions to the imaginary women he creates in the poetry, for they remain sources for his infinite portraits of "virgins" and "whores." Whatever the impact of Williams' father upon him as he grew into manhood, he *chose* (as he told Pound) to emphasize the women, although his important poem "Adam" is clearly based upon the elder Williams.

The remainder, by far the most significant aspect of this study, is the analysis of the development of the virgin/whore as it emerged from Williams' complex vision of women accrued over a lifetime. Herein lies what I feel has largely been neglected by critics. The evidence rests upon an in-depth study of the poems themselves. The choice of images and the poet's "measure" largely characterize a poet's style. That Williams gave to poetry a body of verse in the American idiom was partially the result of image and line and language, but his choice of an American subject and his own *modification* of existing myths "in the American grain" are a unique contribution. The equation Williams drew between women, the imagination, and the poem are all a part of that larger vision of a poem "about America," and complementing this view is his acknowledgment of the "need" for the female within himself: "The female principle of the world/ is my appeal." If he could mold the archetypal myths into American versions of Elsie or Beautiful Thing or the virgin/whore, he could create his own American myth.

Williams accomplished what few poets in the modern world have achieved; he has, as he tells Flossie in "Asphodel," "come proudly/ as an equal." His poetry is timely in its insistence on the necessary interdependence of men and women. Williams' imagination tended to dwell on opposites, but he strained after harmony, concord, conjunction. His hope for reconciliation and consummation was his response to the fragmentation, isolation, and despair of modern existence and as such holds a glimmer of hope for those of us who search for the radiant gist in an otherwise darkened world.

I would conclude that Williams' gallery of women, drawn both from his real experiences and his creative imagination, reflects a more empathetic, perceptive, and enlightened view of women than yet existed in American poetry. Though he protested all his life that women remained an enigma, few male poets have so eagerly sought to penetrate that mystery, and few with such largeness of spirit and admiration.

Audrey T. Rodgers
Pennsylvania State University

Chapter I
"The Whore and
the Virgin, an Identity"

Creative man is a riddle that we may try
to answer in various ways, but always in
vain.... Every creative person is a duality
or a synthesis of contradictory attitudes.
On the one side he is a human being with a
personal life, while on the other side he is
an impersonal, creative process.... we can
only understand him in his capacity of artist
by looking at his creative achievements.

Carl Jung, "the Poet"

I well remember one evening when I was
having dinner with [Williams] in Rutherford
and he launched out on an exposition of his
concept of the "Virgin and the Whore." I only
wish that I had had a tape machine concealed
under the table, as it was most marvelous. Or
that I had put down notes when I got home, but
in those days I was under the illusion that
memory would never fade.

James Laughlin, May 23, 1979
(letter to the author)

Hats off to the lady!

William Carlos Williams,
"Kora in Hell"

At the portal of William Carlos Williams' American myth, *Paterson*, lie the sleeping giants: the Male Paterson ("... under the Passaic Falls/ its spent waters forming the outlines of his back. He/ lies on his right side, head near the thunder/ of the waters filling his dreams! ...") and the Female Garrett Mountain ("And there, against him, stretches the low mountain./ The Park's her head, carved, above the Falls, by the quiet/ river ..." She lies "... facing him, his/ arm supporting her, by the *Valley of the Rocks*, asleep."

The colossal lovers are a pervasive presence in *Paterson*, evoking a harmony and perfection in the once-primitive world and now tragically dormant in the fragmented life of the modern city.

The theme of concord between these mythical forces — Waterfall and Earth, Male and Female — reflects Williams' inclination to view all experience in sexual terms. His lifelong belief in the potential to unite these opposites in love, for even the most miserable human beings, was tenaciously held through a long life of search and doubt and disappointment. The source for such harmony, Williams reiterated constantly, was the imagination that created the language that, in turn, created the poem. This conviction in the redemptive power of poetry frequently gave rise to the association of woman, the imagination, and art in Williams' mind. He wrote toward the end of his life, "But love and the imagination/ are of a piece,/ swift as the light/ to avoid destruction."[1] That "destruction" constantly threatened is the subject of much of Williams' poetry, often posed in the conflict between male and female, but always averted by a "vision" of reconciliation and consummation. The central figure of his major poem, Noah Faitoute Paterson, searches in his world for conjunction, one man "like a city" with many women "each like a flower." This is the quest expressed in the opening of Book I. At times, Williams finds the virgin, at times, the whore. At times, the figures merge in his imagination as a single image, the virgin/whore.

> The whore and the virgin, an identity:
> — through its disguises
> thrash about — but will not succeed in breaking free
> an identity

Paul Mariani notes: "After a lifetime's pursuit, [Williams would] let (woman) reveal herself there at the core of the imagination, queen, mother, virgin, whore.... Not any woman ... but the ineluctable mystery of Woman."[2]

There is little doubt that Williams not only loved women but saw in them both a challenge and a fulfillment. In his poetry he sought to identify with the same life surge he felt women epitomized, what he termed "the female principle."[3] In his conviction that the supposed polar entities of male and female "give birth to a world of becoming,"[4] he found continuity, rebirth, and the cyclical pattern of the seasons in nature and in man. In his earliest poetry and prose, Williams' women were enriched and deepened by his awareness of the myth of Demeter/Persephone. He was haunted by the myth of Kore (Persephone) in Hell. By the time he came to write *Paterson*, he would draw on another fabulous source for his complex portraits of women, the tale unfolded in the 500-year-old tapestries in the Cloisters, high above the bluffs of the Hudson at Fort Tryon Park. The eleven tapestries depicting the pursuit of the unicorn by the virgin would provide Williams with a visual inspiration for his own creation of the virgin/whore.[5] He found in art the models he had already encountered in life, in the "innumerable women" who peopled the busy day-to-day life of Dr. Williams of Rutherford.

Williams' universe comprised many worlds, often in conflict. He wrote in "Shadows":

> ... we experience
> violently
> every day
> two worlds

Living in both the empirical world of the senses and the world of the imagination, the artist envisions himself as the bridge between the two realms of experience—so disparate but so crucial to relate. Through "art alone" Williams believed those worlds could be yoked. At the end of his life he would reiterate the persistent belief that only by uniting male and female, through the medium of art—in the loveliness of the ancient tapestries hanging on the walls of the Cloisters—would those worlds conjoin.

Williams' universe—the quotidian world of the busy doctor in Jersey and the world of the poetic imagination and his "new world" of art (as he termed it)[6]—shared in common the images of "innumerable women," real and imaginary. In the poetry they would assume symbolic overtones, but always they would suggest the infinite potential of reconciliation, a bridge between disparate experiences for the poet who stood astride two worlds and stubbornly refused to relinquish either. It is therefore not surprising to find Emily Wellcome, Williams' grandmother, as the Demeter figure in "The Wanderer," or Flossie Williams the heroine of not only two novels but the "greeny flower" of his finest tribute to love.

Though men had given his life direction, he once observed, "women have always supplied the energy."[7] His personal life was indeed animated by the "innumerable women" in his daily encounters. The earliest were the grandmother transformed into the wise crone in "The Wanderer," and Elena, the mother, who became the centerpiece for so many portraits of alienation. She was the artist, a fragile, thwarted, creative presence in the inexorable dullness of Rutherford. Flossie, his wife, was Williams' Penelope in providing the constancy and responsiblity to which he needed to return after the wild abandon of freedom, the search for the new, the exhaustion of his "seasons of chaos." As early as 1913, he noted his mother's important role in his life: "I was conscious of my mother's influence. . . . her ordeal as a woman and as a foreigner in this country."[8] And of Flossie, who quietly saw him through the now tempestuous, now euphoric, now despairing times, who became his critic and sounding board and bulwark during the years of illness and incapacity, he wrote,

> At our age the imagination
> across the sorry facts
> lifts us
> to make roses
> stand before thorns.

It was Williams' appreciation of her sacrifices and her steadfastness that must have kept Flossie Williams afloat during trying times, when other women would have despaired or cut and run!

He had written, "Determined women have governed my fate,"[9] but he appeared more amused than intimidated by the thought. In his profession he attended hundreds of women in the throes of childbirth, and in the hospitals there was an endless succession of white-robed priestesses who kept order in the midst of the chaos most hospitals generate. Williams admired the "proportion" of these nurses — Sister McGrath, "by no means petite," being pursued by a patient who had been a wrestler; Sister Julianna, "an older black-eyed woman with a whiplike intelligence," was "boss and no prude"; and Sister Elizabeth, "a pure peasant who was shocked when she found I, who could be so nice, was no Catholic. Bless her sweet heart. . . ."[10] He found something to respect in each of them. It was all a part of his generous love for women. He wrote:

> Men are the technical morons of the tribe, women keep some proportion, remain sound even in debauchery, relate the parts to the whole, act, that is with the body, the related parts, together, not a part of it, to be sure, they must to survive. What could I possibly do to them or for them in that complete sense? Nothing.[11]

As a poet, he was frequently pleased with the creative efforts of women artists. He wrote in essays and letters of the gifts of Marianne Moore, Mina

Loy, H.D., Kay Boyle, Kitty Hoagland, Denise Levertov, and other women
writers. Williams' genuine admiration for many of the women who inhabited
either his life in Rutherford or the world of Greenwich Village would have
an enduring effect upon his art:

> The thing that keeps me interested in life after having driven through
> it to whatever success I have been able to attain among my fellowmen
> is, obviously enough, the women. Women still have something to sell
> me.... Women are more sensitive to what Ezra Pound once called
> "the purring of the invisible antennae." ... Even when women are
> old, and sometimes very old, they still retain, if they are aware,
> something I still find worth my while digging for ... the gentleness
> and tenderness and insight and loyalty of women and what they see,
> I am sure, in most masculine looks which should disgust them, keeps
> me plugging.[12]

It is interesting that by the time Williams came to write *Paterson*, he permitted
the women to speak for themselves, and the five books of the poem are in-
terspersed with letters, at times critical and acerbic with no authorial
gloss.

The women Williams knew both casually and profoundly would filter
through his imagination and merge in the poetry with the mythic figures
close to the surface of his consciousness. His poetry is suffused with figures
of Kore-Persephone, Demeter, Venus, and the mythic Helen. They would
reflect the polarities of his experience. With *Paterson V* the figure of the
virgin/whore would serve to reconcile in art what would remain forever antithetical in life. The whored virgin or the "virginal" whore had her sources
in myth and literature. Williams' predilection to find archetypes was compatible with his mythic vision, but his virgin/whore would transcend his
literary models.

Williams' mythic vision reached its fullest expression in his longest
poem, *Paterson*, but it is already suggested in his earliest long poem, "The
Wanderer." Both *Paterson* and "The Wanderer" contain the elemental quest,
the wandering "hero," the recurrent patterns of death and rebirth, the search
to discover the "radiant gist" buried in the common pitchblende of ordinary
experience, as the section on Madame Curie relates, or in the "filthy Passaic"
of "The Wanderer." But Williams' imagination is mythic in a more subtle
way. By means of his mythic view, the poet, as Williams attested, could
realize his purpose "to lift the world of the senses to the level of the imagination and so give it new currency...."[13] By fusing the world of the imagination with the real world of Rutherford, the poet could create his "new
world":

> Think of the work of art—a poem—as a structure ... [the poet]
> discovers and builds anew.
>   A work of art is important only as evidence, in its structure, of a
> new world it has created to affirm.[14]

He believed that "on the poet devolves the most vital function of society: to recreate it in a new mode." The "new mode" would enable the perception of life in the universal moment. He wrote, "A life that is here and now is timeless. That is the universal I am seeking: to embody that in a work of art, a new world that is always real." Williams' great gift was to be able to see his imaginary and real worlds simultaneously and to intermingle them. Women, a life force, would appear in endless metamorphoses. The grandmother and the mother would be transformed in the poetry as Demeter figures, while the sleazy housemaids of Rutherford would take on the tragic dimensions of urban Kores, the violated maiden of Demeter in Greek mythology.

The most remarkable synthesis that would emerge in Williams' poetry, in his new world of art, is the virgin/whore. The image is a riddle of seemingly irreconcilable opposites. It is amusing that this is precisely how he puzzled over women in real life:

> What makes them tick? ... I would draw back from them and try to write it down.... After all, there are only two kinds, men and women, the he and she of it ... I'll die before I've said my fill about women.[15]

The Virgin and the Whore

The long literary and religious histories of the figures of the "virgin" and the "whore" that provided all poets, Williams among them, with images of purity and corruption can be but briefly noted here. To clarify the complex and insistent motifs these terms accrued over the course of time necessitates beginning with their meanings in a popular sense. The virgin is generally equated with sexual purity and inviolability, while the whore is the professional trader in sexual favors, erotic pleasures, for which a price must be paid. The degree to which this latter assumption takes on significance is, in truth, the key to an almost limitless number of interpretations. The dual terms, virgin and whore, represent polarities of many colors: moral, ideational, and psychological. Thus the terms suggest a tension between goodness, virtue, and purity of spirit (as well as body) on one hand, and on the other, evil, corruption, and depravity beyond that of the merely sensuous. Clearly, the ideal is the virgin, and the real (fleshly as well as evil) is the whore, with all of the moral approval and censure those terms evoke. In a related sense, the terms often appear in literature and religion as paired opposites of innocence and experience, sacred and profane. Intrinsic to all these familiar associations with which Williams was acquainted are the themes of changelessness and eternity and transcendence against the contrasting themes of violation, depravity and death. Central to many versions of the relation between virgin and whore is the implicit belief that through "initiation" the pure become defiled in the world of experience.

Significantly, in modern literature that grew from the darker vision of the British and American novelist, the virgin was not "inviolate." In fact, violation seems to have been her fate. Yet in Hardy's Tess *(Tess of the D'Urbervilles)* and in Crane's Maggie *(Maggie, A Girl of the Streets)* an aura of innocence appears to cling to these pure women despite the violation they undergo. This violation is a theme that would not only become an American product but would develop into a major theme in the poetry of Williams — in the raped Elsies and in the vulgarization of *Paterson's* Beautiful Thing.

Equally popular, if not more fascinating, is the figure of the whore who, depending upon how we define her, came to symbolize man's ruin, education, wisdom, and ultimate death. We can note Circe and Greek mythic figures like Clytemnestra and Jocasta, but such femmes fatales as Cleopatra, Chaucer's Criseyde, Shakespeare's Cressida, and Webster's Vittoria Accorombona have been judged to have ruined great heroes. They are the forerunners of an endless number of English and American "dark ladies" who leave in their wake a trail of despoiled heroes. In any guise, the modern "whore" signaled disaster for the man she entrapped, the price paid for the pleasure she offered. She is pursued with the same relentlessness in reality as the virgin is pursued in dream and vision. Critic Leslie Fiedler[16] has amply demonstrated the vigor with which American writers have presented a whole gallery of charming "whores" who bartered for honor, dignity, and the protagonist's self-esteem. As we will find, Williams' whores are more complex and interesting figures who "still have something to sell me."[17]

The Virgin/Whore

> "— the virgin and the whore,
> an identity
> both for sale"
>
> *Paterson V*

The attraction of the figures of the virgin and the whore accounts largely for a third figure that emerged in antiquity and became a familiar image in myth, religion, and literature: the virgin/whore. The term suggests an oxymoron, a fusion of antithetical ideas residing in a single figure. Though *ostensibly* irreconcilable, the polarities of virgin and whore coexist in countless numbers of fictional and mythical women. Although William Carlos Williams' poetry abounds in fleeting portraits of virginal maids (usually victimized by society) and ancient tutelary crones and whores, the virgin/whore interested him as a metaphor that posited many paradoxes in his several worlds and reached its distinctive expression in *Paterson*. "The world itself," Roy Harvey Pearce wrote, "is both 'virgin and whore,' "[18] for Williams could never reject the evil for the good, the real for the ideal. The virgin and the whore was "an identity/both for sale."

Williams had only to think of his favorite mythic figure, Kore-Persephone, to ponder the opposites fused in Greek myth. As Persephone, Bride of Hades, the figure became associated with the evils of the nether world, but as the Kore maiden she returns at springtime, reborn in her inno-cent virginity. The importance of Kore to Williams will be discussed in fuller detail, but other paradigms existed in the figures of Demeter and Hecate and Aphrodite.

It is easy to think of love in terms of polar opposites of good and evil, but neither in myth nor in ancient literature is the interpretation facile. In the Homeric hymn, Greek Aphrodite rises from the seafoam as the beautiful "golden goddess," but Edith Hamilton reminds us that "in later poems she is usually shown as treacherous and malicious, exerting a deadly and destructive power over men."[19] Thus, one aspect of Aphrodite is radiant light, loveliness, joy, and immortality, while her other is mockery, seduc-tion, destruction, and death. Paul Friedrich (*The Meaning of Aphrodite*, Chicago: Univ. of Chicago Press, 1978) sees the goddess Aphrodite as "sex-uality, sensuousness, subjectivity, fertility, potency, and sensitivity" (p. 181). Robert Graves notes that Aphrodite's tree was the myrtle — most often signi-fying death — but the myrtle is evergreen and connotes life-in-death in Greek myth. Homer W. Smith, in discussing the cult of Aphrodite, observed, "In some instances her cult emphasized chastity and austerity but this appears to have been exceptional, for her heterae were familiar throughout the Hellenic period and it was the custom for public spirited citizens to con-secrate one or more slave women to the temple. One day of the festival was given up to the heterae and another to respectable woman."[20] Thus the wor-ship of the "divine prostitute" as well as the chaste women reveals the fascinating quality of Aphrodite that continued into European literature.

Yet it was Aphrodite Paris chose to award the golden apple, Aphrodite who tempted him with Helen. It would be too simple to view Helen as the epitome of love for whom a price was paid — thus the whore. In the be-ginning, Helen is "of fair and delicate complexion, having been hatched from a swan's egg,"[21] as she is described to Paris by Aphrodite. Through Aphrodite's spell, Helen falls madly in love with Paris as all Troy yields to her beauty. Priam himself took an oath never to let her go. Some mythog-raphers deny that Helen was carried off by force or that she rejected Paris' advances, while others believe the real Helen never went to Troy but was carried off by King Proteus under his protectorship to Egypt and only a "phantom" Helen was swept off to Troy by Paris. Certainly some aura of mystery, of Helen's inviolability, beauty, purity, and immortality, clings to the judgment of history. Perhaps this inspired Poe to present us with an undefiled Helen, a goddess inspiring the poet, compounding an already enigmatic view of Helen as both virgin and whore: the figure of destiny whose purity of beauty lured Paris to his fate and Greece and Troy to tragic events. As we shall see in Nikos Kazantzakis' version of the Demeter/Helen theme, she is both a force of life and a force of death: "the round soles of her feet gleamed with blood."[22] The duality of Helen's mother, Leda, is dramatized by William Butler Yeats in "Leda and the Swan," in a persistent motif of the indivisibility of innocence and guilt; the maiden is violated by Zeus in the form of a swan, yet the aroma of complicity deepens the mystery of union. This is still another instance of how a poet molds a traditional myth for his own artistic use.

In the Hebraic-Christian tradition, Eve is the eternal paradox, the virginal temptress who is first lured by Satan and then ensnares Adam in her fate; the price to be paid for his love is eternal banishment from Eden, and death.

Mary Magdalene is the most familiar Christian version of the reversal, the whore turned saint: ". . . she was originally a woman of the streets who lives in sin and vice and who later changed her manner of living, eventually to become one of the most faithful followers of Christ. She is the only Saint who was given the name 'the penitent'. . . . This is Mary Magdalene upon whom God bestowed such great grace and to whom he made evident so many signs of love. He expelled seven evil spirits from her and inspired in her the love of Him."[23] This reversal would appear as a particularly American product in the figure of Hawthorne's Hester Prynne *(The Scarlett Letter)*.

More recently, in the varied females who people the stories and novels of James Joyce the image of virgin/whore contains oblique references to the failure of the church and Ireland itself, where appearance of chastity belies the whoredom of betrayal and self-deception. The virginal figure of the young girl in "Araby" becomes transmuted into the sleazy flirt at the bazaar, Araby. The boy alternately adores Mangan's sister: "I bore my chalice safely through a throng of foes. Her name sprang to my lips at moments in strange prayers and praise . . ."[24] and yields to the eroticism she engenders: ". . . my body was like a harp and her words and gestures were like fingers running upon the wires." Finally, he reviles himself: "I saw myself as a creature driven and derided by vanity; and my eyes burned with anguish and anger"—the price he pays for self-knowledge.

In *A Portrait of the Artist as a Young Man*, Eileen, the young girl in Stephen's early life, is identified both with sex and the Blessed Virgin. Hugh Kenner notes that the "Emma Cleary of *Stephen Hero*, with her loud forced manners and her body compact of pleasure, was refined into a wraith with a pair of initials to parallel an intangible Church. She is continually assimilated into the image of the Blessed Virgin and the Heavenly Bride. The torture she costs him is the torture his apostasy costs him."[25] The "virginal" image of Stephen's imagination becomes the "sacred whore" who exacts an almost unendurable price. Accepting life, in Joyce's view, seems to be a constant assimilation or synthesis of virgin and whore, real and ideal.

In modern fiction the virgin/whore surfaces in such unflattering portraits as Carrie Meeber in Dreiser's *Sister Carrie* and all the lovely daughters metamorphosed into their Jewish mothers in the novels of Bellow, Malamud, Wouk, and Roth. In *Portnoy's Complaint*, Roth's "mom"—the essence of nurturing goodness—sinks to the nadir of evilness and corruption. Novelists like Faulkner and Fitzgerald juggle the images of virgin and whore by presenting Temple Drake in *Requiem for a Nun* and Daisy Fay Buchanan in *The Great Gatsby* ("the first *nice girl* [Gatsby] had ever known").[26] The virgin/whore in most modern literature appears as a morally repugnant though sexually attractive Circe who carries death and destruction to the innocent hero.

One remarkable image of the double presence of the virgin and the whore occurs in a fable Williams knew well and had often seen depicted on the wall tapestries of the Cloisters. So important was the series of tapestries retelling the old fable of the unicorn and the maiden that it became an important part of the thematic thread of *Paterson* and can be traced even in Williams' earlier work. But the theme of the unicorn and the maiden belongs to Book V of *Paterson*, and I shall discuss it in that context.

Williams' Virgin/Whore

> "Pocahuntas, a well-featured but wanton yong girle ... of the age of eleven or twelve years, get the boyes forth with her in the marketplace, and make them wheele, falling on their hands, turning their heels upward whom she would followe and wheele so herself naked as she was ..."
>
> *In the American Grain*

In his *Autobiography*, Williams confided, "Only yesterday reading Chapman's *The Iliad of Homer*, did I realize for the first time that the derivation of the adjective 'venereal' is from Venus! ... I was stunned!"[27] One can smile at the naïvete of the doctor who through the initiation into the sordid and tragic "aftermath of love" during his internship at French Hospital and a lifetime of treating the human flotsam of urban New Jersey could still be "stunned" by the thought of the defiled Venus. Here the poet and the doctor confront each other—the one whose praise for the "female principle" inherent in both Demeter and Aphrodite was a familiar theme in his poetry; the other the physician who daily faced the onslaught of disease and promiscuity, and who would write of "we degraded prisoners/ destined/ to hunger until we eat filth—." The anecdote is interesting not only for Williams' admission of surprise but also for his late recognition of the antithesis rooted in language itself. His own synthesis of the virgin/whore, were it not for the historical models afforded him, might evoke Dr. Johnson's contempt for yoking together by violence the most heterogeneous ideas. T.S. Eliot's retort that "a degree of heterogeneity of material compelled into unity by the operation of the poet's mind is omnipresent in poetry"[28] would have pleased Williams.

As we define the contours of Williams' images of "innocence" and "experience" we find it impossible to disassociate one from the other. In his world they exist with a simultaneity and an identity, losing neither their individuality nor their relationship to the "other." And it is in the image of the woman that the complexity is expressed. He wrote, "When I am asked why I find life worth living, it is the look in the woman's eyes that I saw yesterday which rescues me with an answer."[29] Williams' gallery of women in the world of his poetry returns hauntingly to the figure of the virgin/whore. From the earliest poetry, the associations of the pure and defiled deepen and broaden. She will come to define Williams' view of America, the imagination, art, and love. She will serve to define women as he knew them and created them in the poetry.

It cannot be sufficiently emphasized that Williams' figure of the virgin/whore does not represent the dichotomy between good and evil. It is true that Williams railed at the evils of the world, especially the deficiency in communication between men and women. Williams was sufficiently a moralist to raise his voice when he saw injustice and hypocrisy. But that indictment did not include the individual victims of society who had been used and abused: the Beautiful Thing in *Paterson*, or the pathetic Elsies. He admired Toulouse-Lautrec, who transformed the *poules* of Paris into immortal works of art, and he wrote of the empathy underlying the painter's genius: "I was attracted to Toulouse-Lautrec by his social position which I sympathized with. A whore is just as much a human being as a saint. ... He is a man that respected truth of the design. For God's sake, what the hell difference is it to him that she's a whore? He was indifferent to it, and the poet is also indifferent to it."[30] In answer to a question posed to him in an interview — "Do you think that part of the appeal of the prostitute as a subject is that the prostitute doesn't have to be conventional in the way that a lady is?" — he responded, "Yes, she's a professional figure as a model. All artists are moved by human relations and not artificial, which all the rest of us have to respect. If the ordinary people have remained divided by social relationships, the artist has to get away from that to real human truth."[31] As we shall see, our traditional connotations of "whore" must be postponed as we observe Williams' frequent equation of the whore with freedom from social restraint, wisdom, *truth*, and tutelary power.

In Williams' world, "The pure products of America go crazy!" The innocent, inviolate "virgin" never existed in Dr. Williams' Rutherford, New

Jersey, unless it was the young mother, but even here, as Brendan Gill noted, "Despite his age and damaged heart he was lacerated by sexual excitement; every young mother . . . encountered seemed to strike him as a Venus."[32] More often, his Venus was the lost innocent who might have been chaste in another, better world: "Giants in the dirt . . . that girl . . . the one that should have been Venus by the lust that's in her. They've got her down there among the railroad men. A crusade couldn't rescue her."[33] In the real world of the modern city, the young pitiable prostitutes are the fallen Venuses: "Well, Lizzie Anderson! seventeen men — and/the baby hard to find a father for!" The virgin and the whore converge as the victim of events beyond her understanding or control:

> When they came to question the girl before the local judge it was discovered that there were seventeen men more or less involved so that there was nothing to do but to declare the child a common bastard and send the girl about her business. Her mother took her in and after the brat died of pneumonia a year later she called in the police one day. An officer opened the bedroom door. The girl was in bed with an eighteenth fellow, a young roaming loafer with a silly grin to his face. They forced a marriage which relieved the mother of her burden. The girl was weak minded so that it was only with the greatest difficulty that she could cover her moves, in fact she never could do so with success.[34]

In his *Autobiography*, Williams opens up the world of the hospital and his youthful shock and dismay at the tragic violations he was confronted with there:

> A poor whore came in one morning in an awful state. I hardly knew women and felt tender to them all, especially, like any man, if they retained some vestige of beauty. This woman was round and full-breasted. She has been cruelly beaten. Her eyes were closed, her lips bloody where her teeth had cut into them and her arms bruised and bleeding. But the thing that knocked me over was that her breasts were especially lacerated and on one could be seen the deeply imbedded marks of teeth, as if some animal had attempted to tear the tissues away.

Throughout his life, these early experiences would temper any moral indignation "whore" might have evoked; in fact, he spoke of the dignity of the whore often in letters and endowed her with a transcendent wisdom in "The Desert Music." Old or young, the whores of Williams' real world were objects of pity and compassion. Instead, as he writes in "To Elsie," they express "with broken/ brain the truth about us — ."

So it is that the bridge between the broken Elsies of Williams' real world and the virgin/whore of the poetry is built in the poetic imagination. As we shall see, Williams viewed himself as Kore — the maiden who experienced a violation, a death, and a rebirth that would ensure endless cycles of death and rebirth, darkness and light, purity and defilement. He wrote in *Kora*, "By virtue of works of art the beauty of woman is released from whither it will up and down the years. The imagination transcended the thing itself."[35] Later, in an interview, commenting upon "Young Housewife," he observed, "Whenever a man sees a beautiful woman it's an occasion for poetry— compensating beauty with beauty."

The relation of the imagination and woman always climaxed in the poem, suggesting Williams' equation of the "creative force" with the "female principle." The ease with which he was able to make this assumption derived no doubt from his daily experiences with birth, from his absorption with the Demeter/Kore myth, and from his mysterious equation of woman, death, perfection, and art. He once puzzled over this: "What do I look for in a woman? Death, I suppose, since it's all I see anyhow in those various perfections. I want them all in lesser or greater degree."[36] His choice of the image of virgin and whore afforded him a means for posing the complexities of human relationships as well as life's many contradictions.

On a symbolic level the virgin/whore would bring together the twin worlds of Williams' experience: the real world of Rutherford and the world of the imagination. In the "new world" of art she would maintain all her polarity yet evoke a harmony defying reason. The virgin/whore is a figure or mystery, an enigma, as she was in the classical past; and it is precisely in this sense that Williams is drawn to her. The virgin of his world is not inviolate, and the whore always carries an aura of innocence. The figure, while maintaining its polarity, is nonetheless indivisible. He had already noted the irony of the teenage whore, a childlike naïvete surrounding her deepest corruption, "while the imagination strains/ after deer/ going by fields of goldenrod in/ the stifling heat of September."

In the virgin and the whore he could symbolize all the irreconcilable opposites that formed the sharpest tensions in his poetry: ideal and real; sacred and profane; the pure American past and the debased present; innocence and experience; ignorance and wisdom; joy and suffering; beginnings and endings; life and death. That the land itself was both virginally pure and despoiled by time and technology reached back to the myths of Demeter and Kore, but here in the American context, one explored by other writers before him, Williams would see his America, his Pocahontas, as both virgin and whore. The language itself, as Paul Mariani suggests,[37] is virginal until the poet explores and exploits it. And all of these attributes of ideal beauty and real knowledge, inexpressibly fused in many of Williams' "innumerable women," are embodied in the virgin/whore, the complete woman. These are the modern Aphrodites, Demeters, and Helens: "All women are not Helen,/ I know that,/ but have Helen in their hearts." They contain wholeness of spirit, the "life force" and they become an emblem for the poetry itself: universal, "a new world that is always real."

Chapter II
"Spring and All":
The Myth of Demeter/Kore

It is only in isolate flecks that
something
is given off

"To Elsie"

The myth of Demeter's loss and recovery of Kore had both personal and aesthetic significance for William Carlos Williams, and an understanding of the "innumerable women" in his poetry is incomplete without a sense of the Greek myth that energized his vision of the several worlds he inhabited: the real world of Rutherford, New Jersey, the world of the imagination, and the "new world" of art—the prose and poetry of it. "A work of art," he wrote, "is important only as evidence, in its structure, of a new world it has created to affirm."[1] That "new world" would resonate with the whispered yet enduring echoes of a myth that affirmed the "female principle," that recounted the pain of losing all and the joy of recapturing all, that ultimately unfolded for man the "mysteries" of immortality. The myth of Demeter/Kore, in all its transformations, would become for Williams one means of uniting the disparate elements of his personal and poetic life. If, as Jung believed, "modern man is faced with the necessity of rediscovering the life of the spirit,"[2] then the myth for Williams would also serve his need to extend beyond the urban wasteland, to identify himself with "a purposiveness outreaching human ends."[3]

Williams did not "use" myth with the awesome and scholarly precocity of a Joyce or a Pound. Rather, throughout his work, the numinous presence of Kore hints at the viability of the *anima*—for man "always of immense and abiding significance."[4] Of equal importance, the mother/maiden/moon goddess triad inheres in Williams' portraits of women, enlightens his view of the important women in his life, and reminds us of the pervasiveness of the "female principle" by such poems as *Paterson*. Yet Williams disarmingly draws our attention elsewhere by insisting on his lack of erudition, his penchant for the commonplace, and his general disregard for classicism. We need to listen to what the poet *tells* us, but we need, as well, to attend to his parenthetical asides, his spontaneous hints and guesses. More importantly, we must attend to the poetry wherein, as Emily Dickinson observed, "How still the Riddle lies."

Insisting on artistic roots in the American experience, castigating Eliot for giving the poem back to the academics, distrusting any symbolic reading of his poetry—"No ideas but in things!"—Williams succeeded in charming us to trust the teller and ignore the tale. He was immersed "in the American grain" to the degree that the uninitiated were invited to gloss over the accumulated knowledge that informed his poetic vision and toward which he took a deliberately casual view. In 1922, by his own admission, he was "gathering headway upon a theme of a rediscovery of a primary impetus, the elementary principle of art, in the local conditions."[5] In giving his poetry a local habitation and a name, Williams deflected our view of the past—that "remote past" of which Eliot spoke—from its living presence in his poetry, a bewitching sleight of hand.

I have noted elsewhere[6] that myth and ritual lie submerged in Williams' poetry; a reading of *Paterson* reveals the extent to which classic mythic elements coalesce with the other world, the quotidian reality of Rutherford. Like many modern poets, he quested for some means for "recording and interpreting the personal and universal history of man's inner life,"[7] a function myth has always granted, as Lillian Feder has observed. Driving through the urban sprawl of New Jersey, Williams would sense the "something . . . given off," if only in ephemeral moments, but fused with the imagination that "something" could be rendered into the permanence of art.

It is therefore in Williams' sensitivity to myth—here in the ancient Greek retelling of dying and reviving gods—that one begins, taking the poet's own directive: "To make a start,/ out of particulars/ and make them general/ . . . For the beginning is assuredly/ the end."

Kora in Hell

The birth of an idea often appears casual, accidental, though in essence its source may be traced to the deepest core of the creative mind. In 1920, William Carlos Williams published a book of "improvisations"—the "reflection of the day's happenings more or less . . ."[8]—a total of 365 entries to which he gave the title *Kora in Hell*. Graciously, he acknowledged Ezra Pound's contribution:

> I am indebted to Pound for the title. We had talked about Kora, the Greek parallel of Persephone, the legend of Springtime captured and taken to Hades. I thought of myself as Springtime and I felt I was on my way to Hell (but I didn't go very far . . .)[9]

Pound himself had been attracted by the Eleusinian mysteries evoked by the Demeter/Kore myth, and the *Cantos* contain abundant allusions to this myth of rebirth and reversion and the vision of "Kore through the bright meadow,/ with the green-gray dust of the grass."

Indeed, other poets from the time of Hesiod until the nineteenth century—Keats, Tennyson, and Meredith, among others—had drawn on the riches of the Persephone theme; in our own century, H.D., Lowell, Masters, and Graves were inspired by the image of the Kore maiden swept off in violent and catastrophic captivity by the god of the dead. But it was not until Jung began to probe the psychological mysteries of Kore that our own musings on the archetype in literature took shape. Feder's study of Kore in the *Cantos*[10] is one illustration of the fruits of such perceptions.

In Williams' case, the theme of Kore provided in the ancient Homeric retelling of the myth of Demeter seems to have been imbedded in his imagination for a lifetime, affecting his interpretation of himself, his art, and women—the "innumerable women" in his life, his poetry, and his profession. Elsewhere, speculating on the myth that was central to his rendition of experience, he wrote:

> The legend of the Rape of Persephone or Kora has been familiar to me from my beginnings and its significance to the pagan world. March had always been my favorite month, the month of the first robin's songs signaling the return of the sun to these latitudes; I existed through the tough winter months of my profession as a physician only for that.[11]

Almost every twentieth century poet or novelist has assumed a particular myth as his own, guiding it through its several permutations to that "secret spring of [his] vision of the world...."[12] Nietzsche's observation that "Man today, stripped of myth stands famished among his pasts"[13] must surely have excluded the poet, for whom myth has always served as an artistic scaffolding—an "incandescent focus," in Richard Chase's view,[14]—through which he could experience a fresh awareness of himself and the world outside him. For Eliot, Pound, Joyce, or Camus, among countless others, the choices might be the myths of the Fisher King, the birth of Aphrodite, the tale of Icarus/Dedalus, the myths of Prometheus or Sisyphus, or the Christian myth of death and resurrection.

For William Carlos Williams, the myth of Demeter/Kore was compatible with his artistic vision, so that at the very end of his life he would point to *Paterson II* as a "milestone" and the passage below as "my conception of what my poetry should be."[15]

> The descent beckons
> as the ascent beckoned
> Memory is a kind
> of accomplishment
> a sort of renewal
> even
> an initiation, since the spaces it opens are new
> places
> . . . .
> The descent
> made up of despairs
> and without accomplishment
> realizes a new awakening   :

Now he *was* Kora. Now after a lifetime's testing, summoning up both the despair and the accomplishment, and in the shadow of the final "descent of winter," he could say, "So most of my life has been lived in hell—a hell of repression lit by flashes of inspiration."[16] Ernst Cassirer had observed that man can discover and determine the universe within him only by thinking it in mythical concepts and viewing it in mythical images. For Williams, myth became not only a means of charting his own descents and ascents, but also a way of rendering the impalpable, the ephemeral, the "radiant gist" subverted in commonplace experience into a pattern, a form, an artistic "event."

It was no accident that the myth Williams assumed was transmuted into the "female principle"—as a physician much of his life was to attend death and birth. The shaping of a myth and the use of that myth in his conception of women and in his own view of the poet can be understood partially in his comments on the iconoclast:

> And the way to discover (the way we behave and what we do and what we think) is to be an iconoclast, which means to break the icon, to get out from inside that strictly restricting mold or ritual, and get out, not because we want to get out of it, because the secret spirit of that ritual can exist not only in that form, but once that form is broken, the spirit of it comes out and can take again a form which will be more contemporary.[17]

The central ritual in Williams' experience, in life and then in art, is one of death and birth in endless cycles. Expressed at times as immersion, as reversion, or as descent, the experience of "eternal return" is accompanied always by awareness, pain, and hope. The spirit, however, would be wholly American, but it would emanate from the myth of Demeter/Kore, the Greek paradigm of the myth of the return of spring.

The Myth

According to Frazer,[18] the oldest written form of the myth of Demeter and Kore appeared in the seventh century B.C. Homeric *Hymn to Demeter*, but as we know, it had its counterparts in Syrian, Phrygian, and Egyptian vegetation myths: Aphrodite and Adonis, Cybele and Attis, and Isis and Osiris. All are paradigms of the death and rebirth of a loved one that comes to symbolize the decay and revival of the vegetation in its seasonal cycle.

Though the myth unfolds in various ways, the essence of the tragedy is simple. Kore, daughter of the corn goddess, Demeter, is lured by the beauty of the lush meadow and innocently wanders to gather roses, lilies, crocuses, violets, and hyacinths. Suddenly, the earth opens and Hades, lord of the dead, sweeps her off in his golden car to be his queen in Tartarus. The scene of the abduction, which may have been in any part of Demeter's far-ranging domain, was said to be at Eleusis.

Crazed with grief, Demeter roams the world searching for Kore without success for nine days and nights. Only the moon goddess Hecate's report of hearing, "A rape! A rape!" confirms Kore's fate. Bereaved and angered, Demeter returns to Eleusis disguised as an old woman and gathers the evidence of Hades' guilt and Zeus' connivance in the abduction. Enraged, she curses the earth with barrenness, wandering the world "forbidding the trees to yield fruit and the earth to grow"[19] until Kore is restored to her. Alarmed, Zeus orders Hades to release the maiden. Hades complies, but not before he has tempted Kore to eat the pomegranate which ensures her return to Tartarus. Compromising with both Hades and Demeter, Zeus permits Kore to live in the upper world for two-thirds of the year, but one-third is to be spent in Tartarus as Hades' queen. Demeter's first unbounded joy in her reunion with Kore is thus forever shadowed by the knowledge of Kore's yearly departure for the land of the dead. Nevertheless, she transforms the barren fields to golden grain, and reveals to the princes of Eleusis her rites and sacred mysteries. Hecate, a mythic "double" of Demeter, is entrusted with the task of watching over Kore, Demeter returns to Olympus, and the revelations at Eleusis become the origins for the sacred rituals enacted there yearly.

In one version of the Demeter myth, the goddess, disguised as a crone, attempts to make the son of King Celeus, Demophoon, immortal by immersing him in fire. She is prevented from completing the rite though she cries out, "I would have made thy dear child deathless and exempt from age forever, and would have given him glory imperishable." However, interrupted in the midst of the rite, Demophoon is granted glory imperishable but not immortality. The theme of immersion in the destructive element, here fire, is a theme Williams will seize upon in "The Wanderer" where the youth is enjoined to throw himself into the "filthy Passaic."

The symbolic elements of the Demeter/Kore myth have been explored not only by Frazer and other mythographers, notably Graves, but also by ethnologists, philosophers, poets, and feminists. The most sustained and engaging speculations have come from the Hungarian classicist C. Kerenyi and psychologist Carl Jung.

Frazer believed that the *Hymn to Demeter* had as its main purpose the explanation of the origin of the Eleusinian rites. "The whole poem," he wrote, "leads up to the transformation scene in which the bare leafless expanse of the Eleusinian plain is, suddenly, turned at the will of the goddess, into a vast sheet of ruddy corn." But as Frazer points out, another, deeper mystery is revealed: ". . . as soon as she has transformed the barren brown expanse . . . into a field of golden grain, she gladdened the eyes of Triptolemus and the other Eleusinian princes by showing them the growing or standing corn." The poet, no doubt familiar with the ritual, sought to explain how myth and

rite mutually confirmed each other. The ritual comes to signify the personification of the corn in the figures of both Demeter and Kore: Demeter,
the corn of last year, giving birth to new crops, and Kore-Persephone, the
young corn assured by the return of spring, the mythical embodiment of
vegetation. Robert Graves offers a variation of this version when he notes:
"Core, Persephone, and Hecate were, clearly, the goddess in Triad as
Maiden, Nymph, and Crone, at a time when women practiced the mysteries
of agriculture. Core stands for the green corn, Persephone for the ripe ear,
and Hecate for the harvested corn. But Demeter was the goddess' general title, and Persephone's name has been given to Core."[20]

Frazer's account of the Demeter myth has been challenged by recent
and more "scientific" study of the sources of Greek mythology. According to
George E. Mylonas (*Eleusis and the Eleusinian Mysteries*, Princeton NJ:
Princeton Univ. Press, 1961), former assumptions made by Frazer and such
scholars as Axel Pierson and others no longer correspond with the newly
discovered facts (p. 16). Mylonas believes that the cult of Demeter goes back
to pre–Homeric days (p. 19). He states, "The staging of the event (the
Mysteries at Eleusis) within the precinct could be justified by the belief that
the goddess of the precinct was the giver of plentiful harvests," but Mylonas
places Demeter's realm in Thessaly, and seriously questions her importance
at Eleusis. The "great and unutterable mystery of the Eleusinians, rain—
conceive" could not belong to the cult of Demeter (p. 10). He concludes by
asserting that ". . . we cannot know, at least we still do not know what was
the full content of the Mysteries of Demeter held at Eleusis" (p. 316). Other
mythographers, like Paul Friedrich and Allaire Chandar Brumfield, believe
that the cult of Demeter rested upon the goddess as the "giver of grain."
Friedrich (*The Meaning of Aphrodite*, Chicago: Univ. of Chicago Press, 1978)
defines Demeter's name as "an amount of land under grain" (p. 152 ff.) and
concludes that Demeter stood for plant (grain) growth, the longing of one
for a deceased relative, and maternity, the special relation between mother
and daughter (p. 156 ff.). Among his sources, he cites Arnold Van Gennep,
Paul Francois Foucart, and Jane Harrison—eminent mythographers.
Brumfield (*The Attic Festivals of Demeter and Their Relation to the Agricultural Year*,
New York: Arno, 1981) bases her view of Demeter on her importance to the
several festivals of Proerosis, Thesmoria, and Haloa and Chloraia, as well
as the *Hymn to Demeter*. Her work reveals "a picture of the agrarian religion
of Demeter" in order "to discover why women play such an important role
in the cult" (p. 2). Brumfield would appear to challenge Mylonas when she
writes, ". . . all of Demeter's festivals, except for the Eleusinian games, were
celebrated on occasion of critical importance to the life of the crops" (p. 232).
She believes that Eleusis was the shrine where the sacrifice to Demeter, Kore,
and other women took place.

The several versions of the myth and the confusion attending the names
of Kore, Demeter, Persephone, and Hecate in no way diminished the

richness with which the myth gathered symbolic overtones; in fact, the several glosses permitted a wide range of associations to accrue over the centuries. The resulting ambiguity served the poets well as they touched upon one or another facet of the myth.

In a primary sense, Demeter, goddess of the grain, represents the female principle of fecundity and shares with Kore-Persephone the manifestation of recurring plenitude. If we accept Frazer's assertion that the myth served the main function of explicating the ritual, then she evokes the sacramental atmosphere of the Eleusinian mysteries. Thus, Demeter, as *revealer* of the mysteries symbolizes "woman" in myth: the totality of what can be known, the figure who guides, indeed, lures the hero to knowledge, mystery, and adventure. As the central figure of the tragic drama, moreover, Demeter *is* the universal mother, the "nourishing, perfecting presence."[21] As the primordial mother, she comes to be most closely associated in modern times with the human suffering and pain accompanying the loss of innocent child. Maddened, dazed with grief, Demeter, disguised as an ancient crone, assumes the terrors of reality: "Her bones seem to shrink, her cheeks become wrinkled. She bound up her hair and turned wanderer," Phyllis Chesler describes her.[22] Grieved beyond reasoning, Demeter becomes the earthly wanderer, the exile, barren rage in the face of violation and despair. But Demeter is also power, the unleashed godly power of vengeance and death. C. Kerenyi notes the duality of Demeter in her human sorrow and divine retribution. He also reminds us that in her roles as mother goddess, corn goddess, and goddess of the esoteric mysteries, she is the goddess in triad. This last is the complex significance of Demeter. Kerenyi writes:

> The grain-figure is essentially the figure of both origin and end, of mother and daughter; and just because of that it points beyond the individual to the universal and eternal. It is always the grain that sinks to earth and returns, always the grain that is mown down in golden fullness and yet, as fat and healthy seed, remains whole, mother and daughter is one.[23]

Kore is Maiden. She is always equated with violated innocence, transience, temptation for the gods themselves, and—most importantly—the manifestation of the return of springtime, the "eternal return" of life to earth in the new corn. Kore is elemental virginity, since the primal element of water had given her birth through Poseidon's rape of Demeter, as Kerenyi points out: Mother and daughter are an indivisible unit signifying death. "To enter the figure of Demeter means to be pursued, to be robbed, raped, to fail to understand, to rage and grieve, but then to get everything back and be born again."[24] So it is that Kore evokes death and sorrow, for she carries the knowledge of her inevitable exile to the world of Hades. The brevity of her beauty on earth is hauntingly reinforced by the fate engendered in the eating of the pomegranate. There in Tartarus as Hades' queen, she is, in

Kerenyi's words, "nonbeing." As Hades' wife, she is associated with the evil and hideous manifestations of death. In sum, Kore, the eternal oxymoron, evokes birth and death, innocence and temptation, imprisonment and freedom, beauty and horror, joy and suffering, motherhood and maidenhood. That springtime would always be touched with plaintive sorrow is a theme William Carlos Williams would develop early in his poetry, just as he observed in his daily life that pain was the prelude to the initiation of birth.

Carl Jung, in his classic essay "The Psychological Aspects of the Kore,"[25] emphasized the archetypal nature of the maiden. "It is essential characteristic of psychic figures," he wrote, "that they are bipolar and oscillate between their positive and negative meanings." As he views the Kore figure, she partakes of both mother and the child: "Every mother contains her daughter in herself and every daughter her mother, and . . . every woman extends backwards into her mother and forwards into her daughter." Not only does Kore oscillate between old and young, strong and weak, but between the extremes of goddess and whore. In the male, Kore is the "anima" figure, also bipolar and thus "can appear positive one moment and negative the next; now young, now old; now mother, now maiden; now a good fairy, now a witch . . ." Crucial to the vision of Kore in the poetry of William Carlos Williams is not only the bipolarity of the archetype, "now a saint, now a whore," but also her unique quality of existing outside of time. "When she emerges with some degree of clarity," Jung wrote, "she always has peculiar relationship to *time*; as a rule she is more or less immortal, because outside time." Jung went on to note the presence of the "anima" in the Demeter cult. "The Kore doomed to her subterranean fate . . . afforded the anima ample opportunity to reflect herself, shimmering and equivocal, in the Eleusinian cult, or rather to experience herself there and fill the celebrants with her unearthly essence, to their lasting gain." Jung emphasized the immense significance of such anima experiences.

In summary, the symbolic overtones of the Demeter/Kore myth go far beyond recognition of the cyclic pattern of the dormancy and revival of the grain, though the theme of death and resurrection in nature was a mirror of man's own existence. But other motifs are reiterated here that would reverberate in Williams' poetry: the violation of innocence; the disclosure of mystery that illuminates the destinies of men and gods alike; the tragedy of the wandering exile; the inseparable nature of youth, maturity, and age; the indivisibility of good and evil, joy and despair, mother and child. Even if the loss and recovery of Kore symbolized no more than the nadir of hopelessness and the subsequent transformation to a state of joy and hope, it would have served Williams' needs; he was after all the poet who finally mocked despair, searched for hints of spring "by the contagious hospital."

Both the fable of the unicorn and the maiden (see Chapter V) and the myth of Kore provided Williams with archetypes that bear striking similarities. Both stories deal with the violation and betrayal of beauty and innocence: in one case, the temptation of the unicorn and his subsequent killing; in the other, the capture and rape of Demeter's young maid, Kore, and her subsequent abduction to Tartarus by Hades where she becomes "Death's bride." In both, the tragic betrayal takes place in a field of flowers, an idyllic surrounding of lush beauty but one filled with danger. In both accounts, life is restored: Kore is permitted to return in spring; the unicorn lives again in his wooded enclosure set against a dazzling *millefleurs* background. Both return to life with spring and the season of reawakening life. Freeman suggests that the setting evokes earthly love and marriage; Demeter explains, at Kore's return, the "mysteries" of life in its cycles. But the unicorn is chained to the pomegranate tree, an eternal reminder of death. Kore, having tasted the fruit of the pomegranate before her release from Hades, is likewise reminded that each year she must return to Tartarus to be his wife. The themes of both tales play upon erotic love, on the powers of the supernatural, on the inexorable cycle of death and rebirth. The unicorn fable contains both Christian and secular symbols; the Kore myth is a symbolic retelling of the pagan cycle of death and rebirth in the seasons of man.

Significantly, the central figure in both is a maiden, but the presence of the whore is broadly hinted in both the fable (in the presence of a second seductive and betraying female) and in the myth (Persephone, as queen of Tartarus, is often the cause of death and darkness). The appeal of both myth and fable with their rich symbolic evocations of both virgin and whore would provide Williams with a concrete representation of his own modern concept of the oxymoron: the paradox that had been intrinsic to his vision of women from his earliest poetry. As Roy Harvey Pearce observes, Williams could imagine at the end of his life that

> . . . the poet is now an old man, sure that his has been the right way, that through love for his world (it is both "virgin and whore") a poet may save it from the past for which it yearns and the future which it fears.[26]

Williams and the Myth

"Spring closes me in . . ."

"The Shadow"

In his autobiography, Williams recounts the day on which he became a poet. He collected the voluminous poem he had been writing, a narrative bearing strange echoes of Keats' *Endymion*, Boeklin's "Insel des Todes," and the opera *Parsifal*, and pitched it into the open furnace in the family home in Rutherford. What took its place, he wrote, was "The Wanderer" "featuring my grandmother, the river, the Passaic River . . ." and he might have added, "myself." Williams had found simultaneously his local habitation, his myth, and the theme that "in turn led to *Paterson.*"[27] Here, in 1914, even before *In the American Grain*, he introduced the "female principle" in a sustained work. The relationship of the Kore myth to the female principle is a crucial one that requires definition before an understanding of the thematic threads of the myth in Williams' poetry can be fully realized.

On a primary level, the female principle is the "life force" — the theme of procreation associated with Demeter, whether in the cycle of the grain or in the life of a human being. The recurrent pattern is one of immersion, birth, fruition, reversion to death, and rebirth. Central to the myth is the first stage of the cycle "the descent of winter" with the emphasis on the painful sequence of losing all before recovering all in the process of maturation. Some of the implications of the seasonal death and rebirth of the land are found in Williams' conviction that by a process of metamorphosis the land completes us. The land and the woman merge. Whittemore notes that Book I of *Paterson* ". . . brought the female principle in thoroughly, giving Paterson a woman to live with in the form of the public park above the falls."[28] The female goddess who lies asleep at the opening of *Paterson* contains the lush beauty of an earth-enriching Demeter, but qualities associated with Kore inhere in the portrait: the sensuality, the "beflowered" virginal quality of her, the "nonbeing" of sleep.

> Leaning against the body of her male lover, she is all nature and all woman. The visual beauty of her overflowing bounty awes the wandering Paterson as he observes the male god:

> > . . . his
> > arm supporting her, by the *Valley of the Rocks*, asleep.
> > Pearls at her ankles, her monstrous hair
> > spangled with apple-blossoms is scattered about into
> > the back country, waking their dreams — where the deer run
> > and the wood-duck nests protecting his gallant plumage.

Moreover as Sister Bernetta Quinn points out, the metamorphic principle permits the character Paterson to be both hero and heroine; the female principle becomes a part of him as his imagination, "man's bride, the imagination, figured by the Park."[29] As a symbol of "nourishment" the female figure gives sustenance to the society as well as to the artist. "If a man in his fatuous dreams cut himself off from that supplying female, he dries up his sources — " Williams wrote. Without the female principle there is sexuality without joy, barrenness in women, the debasement of women, a loss of touch with the soul of reality. There is infertility at every level, an observation Paterson makes as he rambles through the world of modern Paterson. Relating this theme to the artist, Williams believed the "ideal" woman completes man, and the poet immortalizes her. This nurturing power for the creative imagination finds its parallel in another writer who also reflects the Demeter paradigm in his work: Kazantzakis in *Report to Greco*. The following passage finds its echoes in *In the American Grain* as well as in much of Williams' poetry.

> Walk along the humble banks of the Eurotas and you feel your hands, hair, and thoughts become entangled in the perfume of an imaginary woman far more real, far more tangible, than the woman you love and touch. . . . The whole earth seems a freshly bathed, laughing-weeping Helen. She was lifting her veils with their embroidered lemon flowers and her palm to her mouth, her virginity constantly renewed, following a man, the strongest that could be found. And as she raised her legs with their snow-white ankles, the round soles of her feet gleamed with blood. . . . It is to the Poet that Helen owes her salvation; it is to Homer that this tiny river-bed owes its immortality. Helen's smile suffuses all the Spartan air. But beyond even this, she has entered our very blood streams. Every man has partaken of her in communion; to this day every woman reflects her splendor. Helen has become a love cry. She traverses the centuries, awakens in every man the yearning for kisses and perpetuation. She transforms every woman we clasp to our breast, even the most commonplace, into a Helen.[30]

Like Kazantzakis, Williams believed the female principle provided the stimulus for the poetic imagination, as it had provided a stimulus for the courageous, sometimes rapacious, heroes who sought to capture the land — always female. The conquest of the new world — in a sense a sexual conquest, a symbol of fulfillment — is the tale of Hades' rape of Kore repeated unendingly in the subjugation of the American soil. Reed Whittemore has described the theme of *In the American Grain* in this way: "Each particular hero has his own particular female body to quest for, but the nature of the quest was always the same. Always the earth discovered and explored was female, with the consequence that the exploration of the Nuevo Mundo was a history of man chasing woman."[31] As the female spirit of the new world offers herself to DeSoto her riches are dazzling:

> . . . I am beautiful — as "a cane box, called petaca, full of unbored pearls." I am beautiful: a city greater than Cuzco, rocks loaded with gold as a comb with honey. Believe it. You will not dare to cease following me. . . .[32]

But the violence of the assault on the land becomes a rape: "Now you are over, you have straddled me, this is my middle. . . . you are safe — and I am desolate." As a final irony, he becomes her possession: "But you are mine and I will strip you naked. . . . Follow me, Sēnor, this is your country. I give it to you." The relentless cruelty of the union of conqueror and the land, however, is not without its harvest. D.H. Lawrence, reviewing *In the American Grain*, was sensitive to the nuances in this unique retelling of American history:

> The author sees the genius of the continent as a woman with exquisite
> sensitive awareness, super-sensitive tenderness and a recoiling cruelty
> who will demand of men sensitive awareness, sensuous delicacy, in-
> finitely tempered resistance.[33]

It was Williams' thesis, Whittemore believes, that "so long as a man was essentially his own man struggling to come to terms in his own way with his own basic primitive self by finding the female somehow, somewhere, he was good, he was authentic, he was probably heroic."[34] Such a good and heroic man was Lincoln, whose "humanity" was founded on his fundamental integrity. Here is Williams' description of him in *In the American Grain*:

> It is Lincoln pardoning the fellow who slept on sentry duty. It is the
> grace of the Bixby letter. The least private would find a woman to
> caress him — a woman in an old shawl — with a great bearded face and
> a towering black hat above it, to give unearthly reality. Brancusi
> should make his statue — of wood — after the manner of Socrates with
> the big hole in the enormous mass of the head, save that this would be
> a woman.[35]

Although I am not suggesting that Williams was aware of Jung's concept of the *anima*, there is little question that his own sense of the "wholeness" of man included the presence of the female principle. Even the whore in "The Desert Music" becomes identified with Williams with "that side of his psyche," which he interpreted as his female self.[36] In speaking of *Paterson*, he wrote, "I was looking for an image to typify the impact of Paterson in his young female phase with a world of his own, limited in the primitive provincial environment."[37]

In his discussion of the "Phenomenology of the Self,"[38] Jung stresses the presence of archetypes as the contents of the collective unconscious. One of these is the *anima*, defined as the image projected in the psyche of the male which coincides with the mother-image but which also includes that of daughter, sister, beloved, or heavenly goddess.

> Every mother and every beloved is forced to become the carrier
> and embodiment of this omnipresent and ageless image, which cor-
> responds to the deepest reality in a man. It belongs to him, this perilous
> image of Woman; she stands for the loyalty which in the interests of
> life he must sometimes forego; she is the much needed compensation
> for the risks, struggles, sacrifices that all end in disappointment; she
> is the solace for all the bitterness of life. And, at the same time, she is
> the great illusionist, the seductress who draws him into life with her
> Maya — and not only into life's reasonable and useful aspects, but into
> its frightful paradoxes and ambivalences where good and evil, success
> and ruin, hope and despair, counterbalance one another. Because she
> is his greatest danger she demands from a man his greatest, and if he
> has it in him she will receive it.[39]

The duality of the *anima* which emerges in Williams' poetry is embodied often in the figure of Kore, who has implications as well for his conception of the virgin and the whore. For our purposes here, it is sufficient to note that the female principle as Williams *consciously* describes it is a nourishing, inspirational life force within the poet, necessary for the act of artistic creation: Mariani notes Williams' frequent reference to the writing of a poem as "giving birth,"[40] necessary as a "solace for all the bitterness of life." Often he would see that principle reflected back in Flossie, in his mother Elena, or in the grandmother raised to mythic proportions. "Men have given the direction to my life," he observed once, "but women have always supplied the energy."[41]

In sum, the female principle for Williams would have both personal and artistic significance, and the motif would often be expressed in the myth of Demeter/Kore, which, in its permutations, could externalize the complex and rich associations Williams found in himself, his world of the imagination, his real world of Rutherford, and finally in the world of art. The women, the "innumerable women," each like a flower, emerged from his vision of the female principle and would illuminate his poetry from its beginning.

It is in "The Wanderer, A Rococo Study" in five parts that we discover the familiar archetypes of the Demeter myth. "That high wanderer of byways/ Walking imperious in beggary!" is the "old woman, . . . my grandmother," raised to heroic proportions. I endowed her with magic qualities."[42] Indeed, she possesses Demeter's power to reveal the "mysteries." The child to be sacrificed to the river, the innocent youth, is the Kore figure who will yield up the terror of violation and immersion in the "filthy Passaic"—a swirling, dark, and degrading Hell in an experience that will precede rebirth. Yielding to the currents of the river, backward and forward, the novitiate experiences the transformation as he and the river of death and of life become one:

> And its last motion had ceased
> And I knew all—it became me.

The poem is interesting from several points of view: the theme of descent is introduced early in Williams' poetry; the "old crone" in disguise recurs later in the Demeter-Hecate figure, here crying out to be ". . . lifted up and out of terror,/ Up from before the death living around me—." James Guimond, in his discussion of "The Wanderer,"[43] has given ample recognition to the Demeter motif that courses through the poem, especially in his identification of the old crone with the dark vision of a desecrated America. He touches upon the themes of immersion and regeneration, central to the Demeter myth, and the degree to which Williams shaped the myth to depict the conditions of his own "chaotic world" and his attempt to assert "a new and total culture." Guimond makes little reference, however, to the unique

identification of the "youth" with the experience of the Kore maiden. Like
Kore, he is "virginal" (not yet having leaped into the squalor and violence
of the "filthy Passaic"); he is sent out into an alien world, Paterson, and finally
immerses himself in a kind of death to precede rebirth. Saved from the
limitations of time, the youth, like Kore, will move toward the certain
knowledge of the indivisibility of the pain of death and the joy of rebirth.
Williams would see himself, as I have indicated earlier, as "Persephone gone
to Hell!" But it is notable that in the poem, *he* is the wanderer; *he* will range
the earth in search of the "new," and the "bird's paradise," and "the secluded
spaces." The poet-wanderer-exile, the grain goddess searching for springtime, moving from despair to joy, from death to life, from descent to ascent,
inheres in the child: as the myth of Demeter so clearly demonstrates, the indivisibility of Demeter and Kore, mother and child, reinforces Williams'
penchant for metamorphosis and transformation.

As some of the briefer poems reveal, he could be the divine triad:
sometimes Kore, sometimes Demeter, sometimes Hecate — youth, maturity,
old age. As Williams drove around the sprawling environs of Rutherford,
the urban desolation passing across his windshield like a modern Hades, he
despaired of the return of springtime. Yet in "January Morning," in the dead
season, he could rejoice at the thought of the rebirth of the land. The happy
doctor (the young Williams crossing the Hudson each day to his life as an
intern in New York) exults as he senses the coming of spring, not yet visible
to those around him.

> He notices
> the curdy barnacles and broken ice crusts
> left at the slip's base by the low tide
> and thinks of summer and green
> shell-crusted ledges among
> the emerald eel-grass!

The poem closes with the poet's eagerness to identify with the laughing
young girls who bring life to the deadness of winter, the Kores of
Park Avenue — those young girls running along the Avenue who always,
for Williams, were identified with the vitality of his own sense of springtime.

In a darker mood, Williams was Kore, the poet, caught in wartime, in
the defeat of creativity by the treachery and violence of world war:

> Damn it, the freshness, the newness of springtime which I had
> sensed among the others, a reawakening of letters, all that delight
> which in making a world to match the supremacies of the past could
> mean, blotted out by the War. It was Persephone.... It was
> Persephone gone into Hades, into hell. Kora was the springtime of my
> year; my year, my self was being slaughtered.[44]

He was also Demeter, suffering through the barren times — times of loss of confidence, personal despair, awaiting the return of his own springtime. As an old man, he would write "in the winter of the year" in a poem dedicated to Eleanor and Bill Monahan.

> The female principle of the world
>   is my appeal
>   in the extremity
> To which I have come.

His aim, often reiterated, was to find the female in himself, somehow, somewhere, in the "impossible springtime." Too many times he reveals, in his conversations, his autobiography, and in his poems, the searing pain of loss, exile, frustration, anger, and disbelief at the gratuitous suffering both around him and within himself and in those he loved. In such moments his mood reflects Demeter's own despair and anger, but in those final years, fighting off the depression of age and illness with a stubborn courage, he retains his faith in that "eternal return" of the "news" of spring — for Williams, embodied in the poem, in art. His faith, at the nadir, returns only when he muses upon the magic conveyed in poetry; for it is the poet in the speaker who affirms the recuperative power of art when in despair.

When we turn to Williams' later poetry, we discover gradually that the myth of Demeter/Kore frequently lies more subtly just beneath the consciousness of the *persona*. We have already noted the ease with which Williams identified himself with the figure of Kore in "The Wanderer," a predilection that will continue in the creation of his major work, *Paterson*. Yet even as a child, Williams tells us, there was a mysterious trinity of the poet, the woman, and the poem: "Somehow poetry and the female sex were allied in my mind. The beauty of girls seemed the same to me as the beauty of a poem. I knew nothing then about the sexual approach but I had to do something about it. I did it in the only terms I knew, through poetry."[45]

As the Demeter/Kore motif became transmuted into the American experience in the world of Paterson, New Jersey, the images of violated innocence would haunt Williams throughout his life. All of Williams' "Elsies" are the unknowing victims of a rapacious "civilization": we meet her in "The Raper from Passenack" who "was very kind. When she regained/ her wits, he said. It's all right, kid,/ I took care of you./ What a mess she was in." She appears fleetingly in "Eternity" in the girl who ". . . had come, like the river/ from up country and had work now/ in town —" But it is in *Spring and All* that the poet brings together the themes of violation and the redemptive return of spring, first in "To Elsie" and then in "Spring and All." That "the pure products of America go crazy" is borne out in the deflowering of Elsie and her transformation into a young slattern. The poem is a masterpiece of Williams'

indictment of the contemporary world. It traces the inevitable desecration
of innocence in the shape of the young Elsie, who comes to the city, falls prey
to its shoddy temptations, and finally is violated by a society that experiences
little remorse or responsibility. Yet, Williams notes, we all bear the burden,
and the debasement of Elsie debases us all. "To Elsie" is a sobering comment
upon the innocent victims of an industrialized society that has lost its direction, its humanity, its conscience — save for vague murmurings of a more
transcendent, regenerative way of life:

> some Elsie —
> voluptuous water
> expressing with broken
>
> brain the truth about us —

In "Spring and All" Williams articulates the theme that out of such death
and decay, "by the road to the contagious hospital," it is possible for spring
to return, and the poet traces the almost invisible signs of rebirth —
admittedly an experience of incalculable mystery, as the " . . . reddish/
purplish, forked, upstanding, twiggy/ stuff of bushes and small trees/ with
dead, brown leaves under them . . ." yield up new life:

> Lifeless in appearance, sluggish
> dazed spring approaches —
>
> They enter the new world naked,
> cold, uncertain of all
> save that they enter.

As I have suggested, the mythic theme of Kore — the rebirth and return
of life to the soil out of pain and suffering — had its counterpart in human
birth, as Williams testified again and again in his experience as a physician.
Death and life was the very essence of wisdom revealed by Demeter: "For
the beginning is assuredly/ the end — " The "event" is a cause for celebration,
and in "April," Williams heralds this rite of spring:

> the beginning — or
> what you will:
>   the dress
> in which the veritable winter
> walks in Spring —

It is, finally, the stubborn human desire that Williams will affirm: the
need for each individual to remember that the Koreate beauty of spring
could return to transform the barren modern wasteland. The "Beautiful
Thing" in *Paterson* who is "maled and femaled" — mauled into the tragic body
on the dirty sheet — can still move the poet: " . . . and I/ attendant upon you,

shaken by your beauty/ Shaken by your beauty./ Shaken." Transcending the corruption and the violence of the modern world, the "Beautiful Thing" still holds out the persistent hope of innocence, promise, and inviolate beauty. At the end of his life, in a final tribute to Flossie, "Asphodel, That Greeny Flower," he could write: "I was cheered/ when I came first to know/ that there were flowers also/ in hell." This theme is an echo of Williams' earlier sensitivity to the presence of the "disguised" gods in his tarnished world. He had written in *Kora* of their ghostly presence, their infinite power and awesomeness:

> Giants in the dirt. The gods, the Greek gods, smothered in filth and ignorance. The race is scattered over the world. Where is its home? . . . It's all the gods, there's nothing else worth writing of. They are the same as they always were — but fallen. Do they dance now, they that danced beside Helicon? They dance much as they did then, only few have an eye for it through the dirt and fumes.[46]

The wandering, ancient crone is a fitting metaphor for Williams' contemporary, slatternly world of Paterson, but more significant is the knowledge that beneath the squalor of the tattered exile lies the power of a guiding force, a mythic reality beyond the grasp of time, inviolate. The old goddess of the river in "The Wanderer," the ancients dancing in the park of *Paterson*, the ". . . old/ squint-eyed woman/ in a black/ dress/ and clutching/ a bunch of/ late chrysanthemums/ to her/ fatted bosoms" in "A Portrait" are all tutelary spirits, leading the poet to adventure and knowledge. Like Demeter they are in touch with the "mysteries" though they roam the world unrecognized. In a slight poem, Williams celebrates that "marvelous and terrible" goddess:

> Yes, there is one thing braver than all flowers;
> Richer than clear gems; wider than the sky;
> Immortal and unchangeable; whose powers
> Transcend reason, love and sanity!

An examination of individual portraits of Williams' women reveals the depth of his preoccupation with the myth of the Kore maiden, but equally significant for the poet is the revelation of Demeter "mysteries." In bringing forth the new corn, Demeter testifies to the reconciliation of all opposites: sorrow and joy, mystery and knowledge, descent and ascent, death and birth.

Book V of *Paterson* is, in one sense, a transformation from the Kora in Hell to the old Demeter awaiting renewal in spring. It begins "in old age," the poet rebelling against the failures of the mind and clinging to memory as it captures the fleeting emanations of a lost springtime.

the song of the fox sparrow
reawakening the world
of Paterson
— its rocks and streams
frail tho it is
from their long winter sleep

Though "Paterson had grown older" he still takes renewed strength from spring and again experiences the river coursing through him, as in "The Wanderer" when in his "novitiate" he leaped into the Passaic:

The (self) direction has been changed
the serpent
its tail in its mouth
"the river has returned to its beginnings"
and backward
(and forward)
it tortures itself within me
until time has been washed finally under:
and "I knew all (or enough)
it became me   .   "

The lines of "The Wanderer" call us back to the past and return us to the present. The divine spirits, Demeter, Kore, and Hecate, hover over the final lines of *Paterson*, as the poet proudly announces, "I give you . . . a young man/ sharing the female world."

Chapter III
From Myth to Reality:
The "Innumerable Women"

So she be feminine, sexed of the heart,
It matters nothing for form or figure
When her eyes speak from the heart

"Ah, Les Femmes!"

William Carlos Williams tended to express all experience, both artistic and real, in sexual terms. As I have already noted, the "female principle" illuminates many of his thoughts on the creative imagination. Robert Macksey, commenting upon the fundamental "oppositions" in Williams' poetry that can be understood only as the "radioactive 'fire' flowing between male and female, between form and matrix, between creation and destruction," goes on to note what Williams' readers have long sensed: ". . . the peculiar facility with which Williams assumes feminine as well as masculine roles.... This androgynous character of his imagination is a clue to the assurance with which he moves from the fury of the 'big she-Wop' and her 'catastrophic birth' to the stillness of the 'male mind, nesting' curiously imitating maternal instincts in the creative process."[1] Macksey then speculates:

> The completeness with which Williams can inhabit the most intimate feminine experience, his ability to move freely from the images of formative masculine desire to the volcanic matrix of motherhood, can perhaps be traced genetically to the profound influences of his mediating profession and the extraordinary women who animate his life — his grandmother, his mother, and his wife.[2]

There is little doubt that William Carlos Williams not only loved women but saw in them both a challenge and a fulfillment. Though he claims women were an enigma to him, he responded to them on every level of experience, and in his poetry sought an identity with the same life surge he felt women epitomized. The disease in *Paterson* is divorce — the polar elements seemingly irreconcilable. But in his conviction that the polar entities of male and female ultimately converge, he finds continuity, rebirth, the cyclical pattern of the seasons in nature and in man as the myth of Kora dramatized.

For Williams, it all began with the two women who competed for him as a child and who ultimately took on mythic proportions themselves: the grandmother and the mother. On another plane, it began and ended with the woman who survived him, the wife who gave him a solid foundation in the normal rhythms of daily life, permitting him to "float free" in his imaginative world when the pressures of being a doctor to the squalid and often tragic lives of urban New Jersey were insupportable.

41

He was aware that the grandmother, "old woman," had "seized me from my mother as her special possession, adopted me, and her purpose in life was to make me her own."[3] He acknowledged the role of both in his life: "Ezra [Pound]'s insistence has always been that I never laid proper stress in my life upon the part played in it by my father rather than my mother."[4] But in launching his autobiography, he says of his early life, "There was Mother, of course, and Grandma Wellcome, my father's mother, the Englishwoman who still sometimes dropped her aitches like any Cockney. . . . At the tender age of thirteen months Grandma took me over. . . . I was in great measure her boy." Williams concludes these memories with the hope that "I take after my female ancestors."[5]

No doubt, the early heart attack he experienced while playing ball at sixteen made the "Twin Furies" hover over him the more, or perhaps it was merely another means of playing out their life-long antagonism. In any case, the event marked the beginning of the poet:

> No more running. . . . But the rest. Not being with the others after school. I was forced back on myself. I had to think about myself, look into myself. And I began to read.[6]

Years later, in marrying Flossie, he chose still another "protector." They would on occasion be Three Furies or Three Graces. How often must he have felt frustrated, suffocated, enraged, imprisoned one time or another by the three indomitable women whose concern, love, rage for order, and jealous attention drove him into the car and out into the Jersey urban sprawl where, through the mottled windshield, he would be free to escape into another world. They sought to dominate him with the unflagging persistence of love throughout his life; yet they never sapped his own strength or his ability — almost feline in its cleverness — to evade them. Whether it was to attend medical school in Philadelphia when New York would have been more feasible, or to leave Flossie and the boys in Europe for a year by prearrangement, or to "steal away" (Whittemore's euphemism for extra-curricular sexual exploits),[7] or to bury himself in his practice (demanding enough!), or in his poetry, or in his visits to the art colony in Greenwich Village, or in his lifelong correspondence with a favored few friends — Williams was amusingly versatile in saving himself from total encroachment. And this for a man who rarely left 9 Ridge Road, Rutherford, New Jersey! Unlike Hart Crane who faulted his mother for ruining his life — with a bitterness that is tragic in its proportions — Williams not only kept a sense of balance, privacy, and humor, but also revealed a deep indebtedness to the "Graces" because, at base, he understood them, loved them, and most significantly identified with them. He *was* his "wandering" grandmother Wellcome, his alienated mother, Elena; and a part of him that savored order, quietness, sense and sensibility would always be "asphodel, that greeny flower" — Flossie Herman

Williams. He wished "to take after" his female ancestors; and at the end of his life he sensed the odor of the old sweet-scented flowers "penetrate[d] into all the crevices of [his] world." The grandmother, the mother, and the wife are each a nurturing presence in Williams' poetry. They give a beginning to a poetic life in which women would assume profound meaning.

Emily Wellcome

"I wanted to write a poem/that you would understand."

"January Morning"

Emily Wellcome was born Emily Dickenson in Chichester, England in 1837, but virtually nothing is known of her natural parents because she was orphaned as a small child and taken in by a family named Godwin. Whether this was the family of the famous William Godwin will never be clear as she was oddly silent about this part of her history. Williams suspected that "she remembered more than she would tell of her girlhood in London in the home of the Godwins whose ward she was,"[8] and so a measure of mystery shrouds the life of the young Emily Dickenson.

In England she presumably married a man named Williams, and again surprisingly little is known about the father of William George Williams save that he died or disappeared shortly after the birth of their son. At the end of *Paterson V*, her grandson reviews her early experience of desertion and remarks upon her strength and stubborn determination to maintain her dignity to the very end.

> She did not want to live to be
>
> an old woman to wear a china doorknob
> in her vagina to hold her womb up — but
>
> she came to that, resourceful, what?
> He was the first to turn her up
>
> and never left her till he left her
> with child, as any soldier would
>
> until the camp broke up.

That she was left with child by an indifferent lover was not Emily's only secret. The other was that she wanted to be an actress — a dream never realized. The young Emily set her course toward the new world with her five-year-old son and her dreams. Mariani believes that Emily was disowned by the Godwins and set out in 1856 with her son William for New York.[9] Today, their journey westward may seem a saga of enormous and courageous adventure. Yet in the nineteenth century, thousands of young men and women undertook the quest for the new continent with a determination totally unsupported by the facts, which presented impossible challenges to unprotected young women.

The trip was turbulent and hazardous as Williams retells it: "The ship was driven by a storm to the Azores and later ran adrift on Fire Island shoal. Pop once told me that as a child of five he recalled being on a deck, in his mother's arms, perhaps, and seeing the bowsprit and prow of another vessel loom above him out of the fog, and strike the side of the ship he was on."[10]

The woman and infant disembarked at Castle Garden, moved to a Brooklyn boarding house, and there met a Mr. Wellcome, up from Saint Thomas to buy photographic supplies. He saw the young woman, married her, and took her, with her son, back to the West Indies. After eight years Wellcome died, leaving Emily with three children and the son of her first marriage. She was one of the multitudes facing estrangement and uncertainty, but after a few years she followed her firstborn to the America that promised so much. Her wandering was scarcely over as she settled in Philadelphia, then New York, and finally on the beaches of West Haven "having there as friends other wanderers, old sea captains."[11] In an age that demanded strong women, Emily Wellcome was bred to be strong. Williams' tribute to her, "Dedication to a Plot of Ground," sums up better than any lengthy biography the indignities, hardships, loneliness that she managed to survive, and quite literally thrive on, for she lived to the age of eighty-three.

Emily Wellcome had the character of a survivor. As Williams wrote of her,

> It has been the passion, the independence and the determination of this woman, born Emily Dickenson of Chichester, England and orphaned as a small child somewhere in the 1830's, that had begun our whole history in America.[12]

Williams was fiercely proud of that independence.

Emily never fulfilled her ambition, but she set her course with surly, proud, and tough determination as she wandered alone. Hard to get close to, restless and resistant, she was a figure to emulate as one who constantly expressed her own individuality.

Williams would later write: "The figure of my grandmother in 'The Wanderer' was semi-mythical. In 'The Wanderer' I identified my grandmother with my poetic unconscious. She was the personification of poetry. I wanted to identify myself with something good and philosophical — with a perfect knowledge of the world." Like Emily, he was the "lost child in a hostile place."[13] Many decades later in an interview he confessed: "I've always felt so lost here, this town, I wanted to get out, I couldn't stick it, so I had to write, you see there wasn't anything else I suppose."

Thus, Emily Wellcome became Williams' earliest muse. He shared her alienation and her persistence. He wanted to write a poem that she would understand, and he wanted to find in this original wanderer the mirror of his own mysterious existence.

Elena Williams

> A serious slender featured boy who knew
> by truth('s) sheer grace his father not at all
> But loved his mother like the breathing air.
>
> "A Tragedy"

The theme of alienation, which absorbed Williams in so much of his poetry and with which he felt a personal identification, was no more dramatically revealed to him than in the life of his mother:

> So in her life, neither one nor the other, she stands bridging two cultures, three regions of the world.[14]

Elena Williams was Williams' Persephone, on the one hand serene and joyous and innocent, full of youthful promise; on the other, morose and moody with an aura of melancholy that enveloped the entire household in a deathlike embrace. "I was really an unhappy child," he wrote Flossie years later. "It was due to the mood of our home and to my eager desires, which no world, and certainly not the Rutherford of those days, could satisfy...."[15] As Whittemore recounts Williams' recollections of his mother, "Her English was poor, her heart was elsewhere, she moped, fell into trances, frightened the children with her strangeness."[16]

She was born in Mayaguez, Puerto Rico, in December, 1847, Racquel Helene Rose Hoheb (the daughter of a French woman from Martinique, Meline Hurrard, whose family came originally from Bordeaux) and a Spanish-Jewish-Dutch father, Solomon Hoheb of Puerto Rico (whose family originated in Amsterdam). As a young girl, Elena Hoheb was tiny, romantic, gifted, and imaginative. Since the family was moderately prosperous, it could indulge Elena's dreams. She was sent to Paris in the late 1870s to study art at the Academie des Beaux-Arts for three years. "She was no more than an obscure artist from Puerto Rico," Williams wrote, "slaving away at her trade which she loved with her whole passionate soul, living it, drinking it down with every breath — the money gone, her mother as well as her father dead, she was forced to return with her scanty laurels, a Grand Prix, a few medals to disappear into a trunk in my attic, a few charcoal sketches, a full-length portrait of herself, unfinished.... Her heart was broken."[17] Elena's dream was over. While the Paris of her early fragile triumph mouldered in the attic, Elena, willful and determined, turned her life to a new direction and her ambition to her children. She had married her brother Carl Hoheb's friend, William George Williams, and began a new life in Rutherford, New Jersey.

Williams was not so dispassionate about the loss of his mother's artistic life. Years later, he would bitterly write in a letter to a friend, Helen Russell, "What the devil are we alive for? When I think of how little my own mother ever said to me about herself and her ambitions I grind my teeth in fury."[18]

In the new world, Elena tried. She attempted a career as a teacher of French and Spanish, but little came of it. She was left at home to the drudgery of household chores, raising children, and fighting with the equally formidable Mrs. Wellcome. Williams felt Elena's marriage to his father was "a house built of disappointed hopes."[19] Her son saw her as an alien in a remote land, and strangely, he felt the same loneliness himself. Childhood for the Williams boys was alternatingly enlivened by Elena's musical talents (she played the piano well) and her painting, and then plunged into the fearful chaos her fits of despondency engendered. Beneath it all, Elena was hard as nails, undefeated, courageous, vain, and unyielding. As in all defeated romantics, a kind of tough persistence belied the nervousness, timidity, and shyness. She lived to be 102 — a determined and independent women to the very end.

It was Elena who brought grace and culture into the Williams' Rutherford home. She led her son to Palgrave's anthology, with its poems of dreamy optimism; she led him to Keats. He wrote in *Kora in Hell*, "She was a creature of great imagination.... She is a despoiled, molted castaway but by this power she still breaks life between her fingers."[20] Like the grandmother, he raised her to mythic proportions:

> I was conscious of my mother's influence all through this (early time of writing, 1913), her ordeal as a woman and as a foreigner in this country. I've always held her as a mythical figure, remote from me, detached, looking down on an area in which I happened to live, a fantastic world where she was moving as a more or less pathetic figure. Remote, not only because of her Puerto Rican background, but because of her bewilderment at life in a small town in New Jersey after her years in Paris. Her interest in art became my interest in art. I was personifying her, her detachment from the world of Rutherford.... She seemed to me an heroic figure, a poetic ideal.[21]

The year Elena spent in Switzerland with the boys (1897), Bill was fourteen, Ed, thirteen. As Whittemore touches on Williams' recollections, Elena "got culture too; she was delighted to be back in civilization away from Rutherford and Pop too. She had a good year."[22] She persuaded her husband to extend the period to a second year in France, where she renewed old acquaintances, sought out her relatives from the earlier days in her "beloved Paris." For Elena it was a nostalgic trip. The return to America could only have depressed her more. She needed success; she was a perpetual dreamer, and her frequent depression can be traced in Williams' cheering letters from Pennsylvania where he was a medical student years later:

> You must be more merry . . . really, Mama, you seem to think that all your happiness is past. That is not right. You have two sons who would die to make you happy. . . . You never talk of your plans and ambitions so tell them to me. I am absolutely sure you often ache to pour out to someone, to lean your head on someone's shoulder and cry yourself to sleep. Let me be your son and brother. Let me hear your secrets. Wouldn't that be just what you long for? Am I not right? I am a man, Mama.[23]

It is probable that Elena never took up her son's invitation; she was a deeply private person (in fact, the sons never found her prized Paris medals until after her death).

Otherwise, Williams' analysis of Elena is sharp and perceptive, perhaps because they shared many of these same qualities and needs; he understood her as no other member of the family could. To them, her fits of despondency were enigmatic and disturbing. But Elena was "steel against steel." Williams wrote, "A woman on the verge of growing old kindles in the mind of her son a certain curiosity which spinning upon itself catches the woman herself in its wheel, stripping from her the accumulations of many harsh years and shows her at last full of an old time suppleness hardly to have been guessed by the stiffness of the exterior which had held her fast until that time."[24] He saw her as an alienated yet emancipated woman:

> A childlike innocence unaffected by age with its maddening mutilations—remains her virtue. To some it is childish, all the characteristics of a spoiled child—which she was—with her bad temper, fears, vindictiveness of an undisciplined infant. To others an indestructibleness, a permanence in defiance of the offensive discipline which is only a virtue to those who wish to flatten out every rebellious instinct down to a highway levelness for their own crazy facility. Be that as it may she has not given in—And still is, as a child, amused.[25]

What emerges in Williams' portraits of his mother is a woman of great complexity and ambiguity. On the one hand, there was the "steel against steel"—the spirit that refused to yield; on the other, the "violated" innocent that the failed artist always evoked for Williams. The duality of Elena reminds us of a familiar contradiction: at once a figure confronting the real world of Rutherford and setting herself against it, while periodically retreating into the world of the imagination, memory, and mystery. Williams summed up Elena's life this way:

> Certainly her life had a definite form and purpose — not by any means sentimental; it was based on somewhat rigid loyalties to the ideal. When she herself was unable to fulfill her desires for personal accomplishment, she transferred her ambitions to her children.... That long purpose, outside of herself, made of her a difficult person to live with.... there is no love lost between her and any other woman that I ever heard of. It is the ringing of steel against steel, the desire to capture the effective male for her uses — high, to be sure! Men! Men that accomplish great things are her ideal.[26]

Even as he knew her, she exasperated him, but he would write to Marianne Moore, "There are times I see her eyes light up with a curious fire.... It clears the atmosphere."[27] In the poem "Eve" he addressed her:

> I sometimes detect in your face
> a puzzled pity for me
> your son —
> I have never been close to you
> — mostly your own fault;
> in that I am like you.

Elena sensed what Williams himself had always known. His preoccupation with her all his life sprung, no doubt, from his identification with her. Almost everything he wrote about Elena Hoheb Williams he could have said about himself: her complexity, her alienation, her iconoclasm, her sheer stubbornness to an ideal, her creative bent, *her* sense as well as his of the artist as an archetypal "Kora in Hell." Like Elena who wanted "... so wildly to escape/ as I wish also/ to escape and leap into chaos/ (where Time has/ not yet begun)" he too dreamed escape. Early in his life, he noted, "I am a pessimist and I must lift myself up by my bootstraps. My mother was a moody person, and her moods affected me."[28] But similarly, he acknowledged that "I have been influenced by French painting and the French spirit, which, through my mother, is partly my own."[29] His Spanish heritage, Townley observed, "seemed to represent to him that streak of wildness, of Dionysian abandon, which his poetry so much needed, and which Williams so much feared."[30]

Even as a very old woman, Elena could remember "on New Year's day, in Puerto Rico, the colored people would come and they would dance. I remember one who had a kind of hoop around him, and palm leaves hanging like a kind of skirt, — dancing his wild dance, jumping and shouting."[31]

Early in his poetic career, in *Kora*, he offered a vision of that free spirit which the young Elena had absorbed: "... the darkies are dancing in Mayaguez ... and sugar cane will soon be high enough to romp through.

Haia! leading over the ditches, with your skirts flying and the devil in the wind back of you—no one else.... Weave and pangs of agony and pangs of loneliness are beaten backward."[32]

To Williams Elena conveyed a mythic sense of the unhappy Demeter in her abandon and her alienation, a creature of dark moods but one whose obstinate spirit yielded to neither the grossness nor the anonymity of life in suburban New Jersey. "Her son," wrote Williams, was "the bridge between herself and vacancy as of the sky at night, the terrifying emptiness of nonentity."[33]

Lame, deaf, more or less blind at the end of her life, Elena received her final tribute from her son:

> She is about to pass out of this world; I want to hold her back a moment for her to be seen because—in many ways I think she is so lovely, for herself, that it would be a pity if she were lost without something of her—something impressed with her mind and her spirit—herself—remaining to perpetuate her—for our profit.[34]

These final comments mirror back Williams' own definition of the "good life" and project values more clearly than any other writing, save the poetry:

> It is in the complexities that appear finally as one person that the good of a life shows itself—bringing all together to return the world to simplicity again; that is her life. An interesting life, because, I believe, in essence it is a good life as she has been a good woman—not good in a sense of being morally virtuous—but perhaps it was that too—but good in the sense of being a valuable thing to me, when I think about it, a thing of value—like a good picture: a sharp differentiation of good from evil—something to look at and to know with satisfaction, something alive—that has partaken of many things, welcoming them indiscriminantly if they seemed to have value—a color—a sound to add still more to the intelligent value, the colorful, the whole grasp of feeling and experience in the world.[35]

He concludes, "if she hadn't been tough, she wouldn't have survived."[36] She did survive many years after this writing. She was tougher than the son who exalted this toughness in his poetry. Williams' finest poetic tribute to Elena comes in "All the Fancy Things." He reviews the facts of her life: the potential of the fragile, artistic girl, her alienation in American society, the pathos of growing old without the joys of remembrance, save a nostalgia for a beginning half forgotten.

"I will write a book about you," he promised her in "Eve," and the fragile book of memoirs, *Yes, Mrs. Williams*, remains not only a sensitive group of reminiscences but a cathartic experience for the poet who, faltering himself, feeling his own strength beginning to erode, valuing the remembrance of things past, joined hands with his mother to make himself whole again, reliving the renewal he had undergone with the Emily figure of "The Wanderer":

But she lifted me and the water took a new tide
Again into older experiences

We can conclude that Elena Hoheb Williams was a living presence in William Carlos Williams' life and poetry. Her life shaped his view of women, his concept of the imagination, and his sense of the duality and complexity of even that which we most take for granted. She was yet another instance of the violation of that which he held inviolate: the artist, the individual, the female spirit.

Flossie

"asphodel, that greeny flower"

They were married in December, 1912. Mariani draws on Williams' early feeling for Flossie from his novel *The Build-Up*. As Mariani writes, "No. He did not love Florence, but he did want to marry her. Marriage first, and then let that difficult flower called love blossom when it would."[37] There was nothing to suggest that the ordinary young girl would become the extraordinary woman whose knack for survival (words Robert Coles applied to Williams) stood her steadfastly through a tumultuous marriage of over fifty-one years. In 1974, Flossie still wanted to "talk about their differences"[38] haunted by the "inaccessibility" of a man whose character, temperament, dreams, and imagination were so different from her own. Yet in many ways, Flossie was the centerpiece of William Carlos Williams' life and art; he confirmed this near the end of his life:

At our age the imagination
across the sorry facts
lifts us
to make roses
stand before thorns.

He acknowledged the realities of age and, simultaneously, the ruggedness of a love that had somehow survived the tumultuousness of marriage and the erosion of time — but only through the support of the imagination that transcended all discord.

Florence Herman began life rather uneventfully in 1890, the daughter of a scrupulously ethical businessman and a social climber who thought her daughter should have made a better match. From the beginning of her life with Williams, the "ordinariness" of Flossie's existence drifted away. His courtship, their marriage, and their life together — the "kid" from Rutherford and the doctor-poet — were tense, exciting, extraordinary except that they spent their entire married life at home in Rutherford, save for a few trips abroad.

The beginning was hardly romantic. It was no secret that both of the Williams boys were smitten with the older sister, Charlotte Herman, "worldly and wise and beginning to give public musical recitals." No one noticed the "kid" when her glamorous sister was onstage stealing hearts and finally running off with someone else after rejecting both Ed and Bill Williams! The choice of Ed had been a momentary diversion to the beautiful and capricious Charlotte. If Flossie ever knew that Bill, the twenty-six-year-old medical student, had proposed to her on the rebound, her nineteen-year-old wisdom chose to ignore it. She agreed to a secret engagement until Williams returned from his year of study in Leipzig. It is a fair judgment that Williams "fell in love" through the mails. He returned to establish a medical practice and after a three-year engagement (protracted even for those times) they were married with little fanfare.

What emerges about Flossie from all accounts of her (including Williams' fictional recreations in *White Mule* and *The Build Up*) is that she knew more than she gave out. She seemed to be essentially cautious, circumspect, private, and practical even as a girl. These were traits that paid a rich return in her turbulent life with William Carlos Williams. "Flossiness" in Williams' novels came to mean a tough sensibleness, family-loving, solidity, and commitment. Even in the early years, Whittemore notes, "He had come to lean on Flossie to keep him from disturbing chores and details and to carry on with normal family life with the steadiness he lacked. By the twenties Flossie was good at normalcy."[39]

At the same time, Williams was developing his idea of the male/female dichotomy. Whittemore sums it up:

> The male in isolation from the female was abstract and imprac-
> tical, was a rootless tumbling weed, and hence needed constantly the
> female presence to keep him from that kind of tumbling.[40]

He grew to appreciate their differences even more with the passing years: the female principle became not only an anchor for his sense of "detachment" from the earth, but a source of artistic fulfillment as well. Flossie supplied that female principle, even as he sought to discover it within himself, much as other women would also supply it. He mused over the conundrum of his love for Flossie:

> For some uncanny reason, you saw through me and you saw me
> good. What "love" is I don't know if it is not the response of our deepest
> natures to one another. I went direct to you through my personal hell
> of doubt and hesitation and I never changed the millionth part of one
> inch since the first decision. . . . I love you and you love me and so only
> at the end will I know what love is — and that is my answer to the world
> and to you. . . . I believe that with love. . . . with love can we dare to
> understand each other.[41]

Yet in a way, they led separate lives, Flossie comfortably surrounded by her friends and family in Rutherford, Williams always running — without her to Greenwich Village to his artist friends — painters, poets, the literary people who were his kind. (In later years, as Flossie came to know more of the literary community, she accompanied Williams on his frequent sojourns to their homes.) A deliberate separation took place in 1927 when, after touring Europe with the boys, Flossie remained in Switzerland while the boys were at school there, and Williams returned to work on his novel *White Mule*. It had been carefully planned; Elena kept house and Williams worked furiously as doctor and poet. There is nothing to betray any emotional break between the two; conversely, his letters to Flossie almost from the moment of separation reveal the depth of his dependence upon her and his recognition of that need:

> . . . the best we have enjoyed of love together has come after the most thorough destruction or harvesting of that which has gone before.[42]

But, as Whittemore observed, "Marriage remains prose and infidelity poetry."[43] Flossie was both innocence of an endearing kind and experience rooted in an acknowledged reality. But Flossie was not the dance-hall Boticellian Venus of *Voyage to Pagany*. Yet, as Williams would write in "Three Sonnets":

> In the one woman
> I find all the rest —

The "infidelity" — what Whittemore calls "stealing" — related in the early years to other women; in more frankly discussing Williams' infidelity, Mariani notes, "The tragedy was not in the sexual encounters he'd had, finally, but in the dawning realization that he would never be able to eradicate the hurt he'd done her nor the hurt he himself felt at having hurt her."[44] "Stealing" referred as well to Williams' escape from Flossie's prosaic world — Rutherford, the babies, the shopping, the neighbors, the friends — to the world of the imagination (two worlds William Pritchard claims were not to be bridged). He wrote to Marianne Moore in 1921:

> . . . each must free himself from the bonds of banality as best he can; you or another may turn into a lively field of intelligent activity quite easily, but I, being perhaps more timid or unstable at heart, free myself by more violent methods.[45]

Those "violent methods" as Pritchard notes,

> would be designed to remove any notions of a comfortable suburban atmosphere the reader might have begun to intuit from his early

poems, as well as removing from the scene the doctor-poet who had not been averse to contemplating himself. In general the new work would disabuse us of notions about an easy continuity between life and art.[46]

In his poem "To Daphne and Virginia," Williams mused on the need for his freedom from Flossie's constraints: "My love encumbers me." He complains about the difficulty of giving and taking that he knows are intrinsic to marriage, and admits there are times he longs for "freedom."

Both Williams' letters and his autobiography make clear that his escape to the Village—the world of Marsden Hartley, Charles Sheeler, Charles Demuth, Alfred Kreymborg, Walter Arensburg, and others—was his major "infidelity" to Flossie's prosaic world. As for Flossie, she never ran away; she made the necessary fullest commitment. Williams' amusing poem "The Thinker" is his grateful appreciation for her steadfastness. Tongue in cheek, Williams associates all that is Flossie with her pink slippers: clean, gay, comforting, a wellspring of happiness and security. The poem is a universal favorite, the image homely and familiar. Here is Flossie, as in the greeny asphodel, neither exotic nor mysterious, but the necessary adjunct to a life that carried its own self-doubt, anxiety, restlessness, and alienation. Flossie's pink slippers are a metaphor for Williams' lifeline of normalcy, and, he says,

> I talk to them
> in my secret mind
> out of pure happiness.

The year they spent apart is proof that the "differences" fed their love. He missed her, but he needed the isolation, the freedom, to write the poetry. Yet from a distance he could write his hymn of devotion and love. He could imagine love as a constantly dying and reviving process, surmounting his "stealing." In an early poem to Flossie (in 1927), he wrote,

> Christ I have
> lied to you about
> small things
>   whoring and
> whatnot
>   but never
> did I unknow that your love
> is in me and I
> in it

As late as 1939, he wrote about his love for Flossie to Robert McAlmon:

But Floss is worth having lived to discover—and she to have lived through it for me. The damned kid is in better health of late than

formerly and, when she isn't cursing me to hell for my bad habits, does
everything in her power to make life worth living in every way for me.
I'd like to give her a break before we both die of this or the other. . . .[47]

There were many years left for them to share and suffer and endure.
While in his early years he was convinced he needed other women in addition
to Flossie, "needed the female principle," the years of work and illness and
the increasing burden of literary recognition made him grateful to lean on
Flossie. She came to know his closest friends well — Kenneth Burke, James
Laughlin, and Robert McAlmon, among others. She helped him with his
work, researching history for both *In the American Grain* and *Paterson*. She pro-
tected him from both his friends and enemies, at times fiercely. She managed
his finances, offered her own critical views. He wrote to James Laughlin,
"Floss looked it over and gave me the green flap. . . . Now I got the story
which Floss says is one of my best and I've also got the satisfaction of feeling
I can still do it."[48] Finally, she was his nurse over the long years of struggle
against the vestiges of stroke. As Whittemore notes, "The nursing commitment for WCW's last decade was enormous and could have destroyed them
both if the love commitment had not been as great."[49] Williams' love for
Flossie shines through the letters as well as the last poems. He wrote to
Laughlin from Greece in 1945:

> Floss sends a smile and a curl from her lovely
> grey head of hair. I get a big kick out of seeing
> her look ten, fifteen years younger under this sunlight.[50]

He paid his greatest tribute to Flossie in two poems written toward the end
of his life: "The Ivy Crown" and "Asphodel, That Greeny Flower"; but as
early as 1911 he chose her as his subject in a traditional love song that
overflows with Renaissance freshness. Published by Flossie in 1974, it was
printed as the "Christmas Broadside #7" by the Lockwood Memorial Library.
It is an interesting contrast with the love poetry of the older, pain-ridden
poet. The poem is a celebration — a song of praise from a knight to his lady.
Though they are separated, she is yet his strength and his life source. No
poem in Williams' canon bears the slightest resemblance to the medieval tone
of this song. Lyrical in its form with the accent on incremental repetition and
a fixed stanzaic pattern, the poem is cavalier in spirit and romantic as the
poet sets his song against the blowing wind and the pang of separation.

Much later in his life, more sensitive to the struggles through which he
had come over the long years of their marriage, yet still reaffirming the
triumph of love over inconstancy, he would assert in the poem "To Be
Recited to Flossie on Her Birthday":

> that tortured constancy
> affirms
> where I persist

For the poet who could express precisely his need for the female principle, he still wrestled with the most perplexing task of all: to explain to Flossie the nature of his love for "you whom I love/ — and cannot express what/ my love is, how it varies, though/ I waste it — ." The birthday poem is one of many attempts Williams made during a long life that struggles to express the inexpressible; his love, despite all the vagaries of his actions, remained deep and abiding. If ever Flossie had her doubts, these several poems lived as a permanent testament to his love.

"Innumerable Women"

> ... I
> who loves them,
>   loves all women ...
>
> "To Daphne & Virginia"

Given Williams' view of the relationship between the imagination, women, and poetry, it is unlikely he would have been oblivious to the beauty, sexuality, and vivacity of women. Given his profession, he came to know them more intimately than most men. There is almost a boyish wonder and enthusiasm he exhibits in the presence of the female principle that serves to mediate, if not excuse, his "stealing" away to other women. In an interview, he noted about "The Young Housewife," "Whenever a man sees a beautiful woman it's an occasion for poetry—compensating beauty with beauty."[51]

Townley, among other critics, has noted, "Flowers, poems, and women are closely related for Williams. All three represent perfect beauty, contain secrets and generative mysteries, and combine delicacy with great hardiness and power."[52] I have already noted the importance of the regenerative nature of the Demeter myth to Williams, and he easily made the transformation from nature to life to poetry. Townley comments on

> The "deeper mind"—the faculty of making profound connections.
> Trees begin to flower, the flower becomes a poem, a poem is a dance,
> the dance is a woman, the woman is in the man, the man is a poet,
> the poet becomes a tree.[53]

The tree is of course the many trees in Williams' poetry that connote strength, cyclic generation, beauty, mystery, complexity, and delicacy.

To his wife, he needed to confess, and wring from her the understanding and forgiveness another poet, Robert Burns, had won. The poem is confessional in nature. The poet admits the tantalizing attraction for all that is feminine. The explicit comparison with Bobby Burns carries an implicit plea for forgiveness, and the disarming identification of the mature poet with the young Irish bard adds a note of mischief to the poem. Time after time, he would invoke Flossie's understanding just as Burns' Jean

> . . . forgave him
> and took him to her heart
> time after time
> when he would be
> too drunk
> with Scotch
> or the love of other women

The poem is one of Williams' many acts of contrition to Flossie, asking her in the later years for forgiveness for early lapses and reassuring her that despair and the need for the "female" and the need to write the poem were all to forget himself. The humorous twist at the end gives the poem the distancing that reminds us again of the old man speaking through the old woman, placing in perspective the insignificance of early indiscretions.

The only poem in Williams' canon that betrays his joy in illicit love and the transforming effect upon him is the little known "Rain." It is honest, while at the same time romantic and full of the lusty enjoyment of sexual love that we find in the poetry of Theodore Roethke.

While it is not the purpose of this study to catalog the women who played a romantic role in Williams' life, it is important to mention one or two of the women who contributed to his notions about the mystery of sexuality, his creation of the virgin and the whore in his poetry, and the nameless, faceless women patients who gave him the most important gift of all—the intimacy of childbearing that went so far toward his essential belief in the female principle.

Williams met two young women through his friend Ezra Pound when both were studying at Penn in the early days. The first was H.D. (Hilda Doolittle) who supposedly was Ez's girl, but from the beginning Williams and H.D. formed a lifelong friendship that was never a romantic involvement. In 1906 he wrote about H.D., "She is a fine girl, no simple nonsense about her, no false modesty and all that, she is absolutely free and innocent."[54] Williams had met his first important "virgin," and his affection for H.D. persisted as his admiration for her grew: "I like Hilda very much. H.D. was studying Greek by herself when I first met her. She was a freshman at Bryn Mawr, in the same class as Marianne Moore."[55] Thus, quite early in his life Williams met women poets who challenged him to follow their artistic development throughout his life. He was always interested in the experiments of other poets, and though he thrashed Eliot in public, he was amazingly objective and clear-minded about the poetic accomplishments of H.D. and Marianne Moore. His tribute to Moore rests on an acute observation that is a central element of the criticism of her work: "Miss Moore gets great pleasure from wiping soiled words or cutting them clean out."[56] His championship of women poets included Kay Boyle, Marcia Nardi, and Mina Loy. He wrote of Moore and Loy:

> Of all those writing in America at the time she was here, Marianne Moore was the only one Mina Loy feared. By divergent virtues these two women have achieved freshness of presentation, novelty, freedom, a break with banality.[57]

But perhaps his greatest tribute was made to Denise Levertov, with whom he felt a particular empathy.

> She is half Welsh and half Jewish. That's a curious thing and must have its influence on her poetry. . . . I feel closer to her than any of the modern poets. She is more alert — very much more alert to my feeling about words — As Flossie says, she is America's woman poet of the future.[58]

But the "first love" of Williams' early life was Viola Baxter. He wrote to her in 1910 (two years before his marriage to Flossie):

> There is something magical about you and yet not entirely fairylike. It riles me and frankly, makes me think more of imps and angels, but even here you have no exact counterpart.[59]

According to Whittemore, his infatuation with Viola Baxter was passionate but short-lived. Mariani would appear to dispute this in his careful tracing of the Viola relationship over a period of almost 20 years. "Tortuous, dramatic, and frustrating in the extreme" is one way Mariani characterized a stage of Williams' relationship with Viola.[60]

Viola Baxter Jordon was the second woman to meet Williams through his friendship with Ezra Pound, in 1907. She was everything Flossie was not: sophisticated, "non-Rutherfordian," beautiful, and witty. The series of letters Williams wrote to Viola trace the development of their friendship. The tone changes from passion to camaraderie. The letters touch upon the inequality between men and women, the complex nature of sexuality, paeans of praise for Flossie's virtues, the rewards of chastity (tongue in cheek), Viola's low estimate of herself, and an endless set of ruminations on the magnetic subject of "love." In one letter he writes:

> Liebe Viola: —
> Mude bin ich — abervorwarts to — the Repellant Flame is merely love, always active, never to be denied. Men know it as babies know the mother — as a place. (I mean men and women.) It is a force which can be felt, it is multiform — I have felt it to command me in opposite ways now and then, that its purpose be accomplished. It has larger purposes and small purposes it has favorite purposes — all mysterious.

> One counteracts upon the other. Then love is a repellant flame which
> can only be denied at the expense of all satisfying accomplishment — or
> else results barrenness. Love will have his way.
>
> (Dec. 1, 1911)[61]

In 1918 he was still writing fictionally about Viola:

> Once I had a beautiful friend whom I loved and who loved me. It was
> not easy for us to see each other, every moment that we would spend
> together having to be stolen.[62]

By 1913, the passion had cooled to be transformed by a warm friendship that
lasted many years. Compared to Viola, the women Williams later found
were less beautiful and of a lower state. They are succinctly present in "Arrival." Of all Williams' confessional poems, this is the most explicit. We
follow him to the forbidden room and the temptation of the "tawdry body."
Yet there is a delicacy in the poem — in the stealth of the lover, the "silk and
linen leaves" of autumn, and the twisting form imaged in the wintry wind.
As always in Williams' poetry, beauty and tawdriness are intermingled.

Joseph Riddel, in discussing the Homeric strain in Williams' poetry as
opposed to the Orphic view, emphasized the "song of loss" in Eurydice's
ravishment in the Orphic myth: the "whoring of the virgin" a source of "the
inevitable failure of man's attempt to recapture a lost presence," while the
Homeric view recognizes and accepts the "loss of plenitude" and the "violence
that lies in all origins."[63] Yet the Homeric view recognizes as well the poet's
need to recover the whored virgin, accepting history "because he accepts the
initial violation which launched him into time." Riddel notes that Williams' poetry is distinguished by his embracing the paradox of the whored
virgin.

It is perhaps this view that drew Williams to the despoiled and tragic
women of this world: the girls who tried to kill their illegitimate infants
before they could be recovered, the young whores hidden away in dirty tene-
ment rooms or loitering near the factories. The archetypal whore is the figure
of the Baroness Elsa Freytag Von Loringhoven, whom Williams describes
as a "fabulous creature well past fifty,"[64] former protégée of Marcel Duchamp,
and denizen of the Village. (Mariani describes her as "the hag-ridden soul
of a potentially decadent America in the flesh, living in a filthy and disgusting
cold-water flat in the city.") "The Baroness reminds me of my gypsy grandmother, old Emily," he wrote, "and I was foolish enough to say I loved her."
The account of the baroness is a hilarious episode in Williams' extracur-
ricular exploits. At first he had called on her, given her money. "We talked
and that was all. We talked well and I was moved." But she pursued him to
Rutherford and became so violent that he summoned the police. The crazed
old whore nonetheless touched a sympathetic chord in him, even as the
police led her away. He wrote:

It was funny to see her walking down the street trying to take hold of Officer Campbell's arm and he pushing her away. I was really crazy about that woman. Later I gave her $200 to get out of the country. It was stolen by the go-between. I gave her more and finally she went, only playfully killed by some jokester, it is said, who turned on the gas jet in her room while she was sleeping.[65]

In a rather loosely organized, unpublished essay entitled "The Baroness Elsa Freytag Von Loringhoven," Williams speculates on the nature of friendship, sex, and love. Some of his musings enhance our other accounts (as Mariani's, above) of the phenomenon of the baroness:

It has been first with me to find out what life means and though I have got nowhere it does not mean sex — not in my experience. Nor apparently in the case of the Baroness.

Men I have found insignificant to me, interested in fire-engines or — that. Women I have found tremendous, absorbed in the body of their opponent, real.

So I truthfully say that every love is the aroma and the fires of one love. We say "she." It expressed what — all I am willing or care to say. She is there.... I run from here when her image which I saw once in inspiration and had photographed on my spirit, a purity I never had equalled in me.

Women — have a physical importance to me, quite apart from what they might turn into for my particular meeting. Men are obviously unimportant.[66]

These fragmented meditations reveal an interesting counterpart to Williams' concept of the virgin and the whore: how frequently the discussions of the baroness combine the tawdry, darker side of the aging nymphomaniac with a kind of experience and tough purity that remained within her, if only in vestigial form. It is the baroness who appears and reappears in the later poetry of William Carlos Williams and who comes to represent not merely a violation of the spirit, but the fruits of experience in the harsh real world.

In many respects the patients he ministered bore the physical manifestations of the same destroyed inner spirit. On one occasion, Whittemore writes,

WCW knew what he was about now, and treated his patients with ease and rough love, admiring them not for their beauty and virtue but for their ills, for "every distortion to which the flesh is susceptible, every disease, every amputation."[67]

Williams himself declared in 1934, "I'm very much physician — tearful mothers, etc. And I fall for it, time after time. What makes that? Feel sorry for the poor bastards — while they're killing me slowly, robbing me of my precious time, interrupting my spurts. I must be crazy."[68] He wasn't "crazy." He was as much drawn to their misery and tragedy as to the Sirens' call to isolation and the creative effort. They were the America he would transform into poetry, and always they were women. Always the world discovered and explored and recovered would be female.

Chapter IV
The Emerging Image:
Women in Williams' Shorter Poems,
1910–1950

"It is the woman in us
That makes us write —"

"Transitional"

At sixteen, when a sophomore at Horace Mann High School, Williams suffered a collapse while preparing for a track meet; the "adolescent heart strain"[1] resulted in the end of his running career and several months of enforced rest. The event may well have altered his life in an indescribable way, for the previous boyish activity gave way to an unforeseen pause that, from boredom alone, made him seek quieter activities. He tried painting and poetry.

As he tells us in his autobiography, "My first poem was born like a bolt out of the blue. It was unsolicited and broke a spell of disillusion and suicidal despondency."[2] This was in 1900; the poem is a brief image of despair and anger:

> A black, black cloud
> flew over the sun
> driven by fierce flying
> rain.

"From that moment I was a poet," Williams wrote. Thus from about seventeen until his death in 1963, when he left unfinished the sixth book of *Paterson*, Williams wrote poems almost uninterruptedly. For over sixty years, despite his busy career as medical doctor, friend to painters and poets, writer of novels and plays and endless numbers of letters, and modern "Don Quijote in a Model-T,"[3] Williams completed a large body of poetry that only today is undergoing full and serious study and evaluation. Critics have seized upon Williams' poetry in an effort to determine the course of his artistic development, and it is evident that the poet changed his views on technique and the nature of poetry itself over the years.

Williams experimented with the possibilities of the image — a result no doubt of his earlier poetic debates with Ezra Pound and H.D. while at Penn. He wrestled with the verse line, not wholly satisfied with the "new freedom" espoused by other poets. He wrote in "This Florida: 1924": "And we thought to escape rime/ by imitation of the senseless/ unarrangement of wild things—" He experimented with forms, but most importantly with language itself, seeking to penetrate the latent possibilities in the spoken language and yet sensitive to the precise and fine-tuned quality of the "right" words. He caught in snapshot form a single image of beauty or sordidness or despair or joy; yet in sustained poems like *Paterson* and "The Desert Music" he brought together not only an American myth and an American idiom, but a new version of the "open poem"—on the surface fragmented but containing a submerged scaffold and a consistent theme. He built a collage of images that possessed all the power and precision of a great mosaic, each piece individualized and sharp, forming the artistic whole as in *Paterson* of a modern drama: narrative, character, action, theme, and form subtly built into a unity. It is therefore possible to trace these aspects of Williams' artistic development as the man and the poet matured over the years.

In other respects, however, certain recurrent themes and images haunted Williams all his life, and, though appearing in countless variations, occurred at the very beginning of his poetic career and held him captive to the very end. One theme was America itself and his "quarrel with that world": the ugliness of the urban wasteland; the indifference to human pain and despair; the failure in communication; the loss of America's purity and youth; the "rape" of the land; the crassness of American values with their emphasis on money and "grab"; the insensitivity to art and language; the lack of love everywhere. He knew America needed to recover its lost pride and its lost sense of direction, but there seemed to be "No one/ to witness/ and adjust, no one to drive the car." Like Frost, he knew the potential was there to recapture the first beauty, and he glimpsed it often in the faces of young women, a kind of radiant glow that lifted his heart. The answer was not in Europe, nor in some esoteric or academic route, nor in religion. The answer was in the poet, the imagination, the language. And the answer was in "woman." She symbolized the regenerative principle: the life force that was part of the land itself, in Pocahontas, and he sought her as he searched for renewal in the female earth. The answer for most of us who were not poets, Williams acknowledged, was in love, in the communion of the sexes and in a generous acceptance that only together are we whole.

It is therefore not surprising that from the very first poems, Williams' "innumerable women" play a significant part in a body of poetry that reflected his view of the relationship of the imagination, women, and art. The prosaic world was his mine of experience, and his intimate association with women patients, the early effect of his mother and grandmother, the lifelong companionship with Flossie, his wife, and his friendships with other women—many of whom, as we have seen, were poets and writers themselves—all reveal his genuine admiration for women and his indebtedness to them. They were tutelary spirits, erotic and therefore ever-dangerous temptations, calming and comforting havens from the giants of despair and *ennui*, objects of pure beauty, and both virgin and whore. Whether in imagistic snapshots or sustained portraits, Williams' women are inseparable from his creative imagination, and to the end of his life he sought to unite himself with the life force they symbolized and to make it permanent in art. He reveals this when he speaks of another artist, Matisse:

> There she lay and her curving torso and thighs
> were close upon the grass and violets.
> So he painted her. The sun had entered his head in the color
> of sprays of flaming palm leaves.... She had chosen the
> place to rest and he had painted her resting ...
> — Here she lay in this spot today not like Diana or Aphrodite
> but with better proof than they of regard for the place she
> was in. She rested and he painted her.
>   It was the first of summer. Bare as was his mind of interest
> in anything save the fullness of his knowledge, into which
> her simple body entered as into the eye of the sun himself,
> so he painted her.[4]

In many ways, Williams' early women are small sketches, paintings of women who filled his mind as he hurried through his busy days as a doctor, but always recording the moments of beauty or pity or temptation as they crossed and recrossed his path.

> "Through what extremes of passion
> had you come, Sappho, to the peace
> of deathless song?"

Poems: 1910–1936

In an amusing poem written circa 1901, "Ah, Les Femmes!" Williams makes his first tribute to the paradoxical nature of women. Tongue in cheek, he accepts all differences. Recognizing the polarity in woman — "Holy or hellish," or both simultaneously — Williams saw in woman that "infinite variety" of a Cleopatra. She banishes terror, confusion, and discord "when her eyes speak from the heart." This is one persistent theme that appears early in Williams' many-faceted images of women. They could always move him, often to deep emotions. As late as *Paterson*, seeing the broken body of the Beautiful Thing, mauled on the bed, he is deeply stirred:

> — for I was overcome
> by amazement and could do nothing but admire
> and lean to care for you in your quietness —

They smile at each other as, overcome by mixed emotions of awe and admiration, the poet-doctor finds himself shaken by her beauty. Those emotions often recur in Williams' poetry: shaken, overcome, amazed.

In a group of poems that appear in *The Tempers* (1913), these motifs begin to appear, as well as other recurrent images. At times, in single portraits of women, he records the temptation to capture forever the transient youthful beauty as a way of transcending the ugly prosaic existence around him. Williams notes the inevitability of injured innocence, but he returns again and again to woman as a synthesizing figure. One dominant theme of the early poems in this volume is eroticism, not merely for the sake of the pleasurable experience, but intensified by an awareness of death and life — Donne's and Marvell's theme. Life is more often understood through the sensuous than through the spiritual. Williams had said he would lift the world of the senses to the level of imagination; and in "Postlude" the speaker moves from the stasis following lovemaking to a hymn evoking other lovers in antiquity. In a song to reawaken the cooled passions, he invokes the deities worshiping at the Temple of Isis to arm the lovers against the hostile stars that "swarm to destroy us." He addresses himself to Sappho, who harmonized all disparities: love and war (Venus and Mars), Carthage's destruction and the echo of its greatness which lives in the shards of the ruined temples. The poet will bring together life and death, sun and stars. The poet-speaker is another Jason on a journey of discovery, but the inner quest seeking union in rite concludes with prayers to the pagan gods and the promise of rebirth after the experience of death.

In this early poem Williams sees love as both giver and destroyer ("Who wounded me in the night"), birth and death. The male is both violator and "war-ravaged"; the aftermath of love is a kind of peaceful death ("Calm in Atlantis") as again Williams plays upon Donne's theme of death and climax. Clearly, the woman merges with all temptresses of antiquity and contains the power to conquer him with her sexual beauty, offering him a means to confront the forces that swarm to destroy them. "Postlude" is a complicated and enigmatic love song; Williams will often invoke the gods and goddesses, but here his awareness of their duality reflects his own ambiguity about innocence and experience.

"First Praise" is another poem that combines erotica with the universal theme of woman as earth figure, as life-giver. The title again suggests homage and is a rather traditional lyric that hints at the virgin birth, Williams' own reverence for his "Lady," and the mixture of sexual and spiritual. The Demeter figure evokes the theme of life-giver in the "dusk-wood fastnesses,/ . . . the crisp, splintering leaf-tread," and the "Lady of rivers strewn with stones." He searches for her, unites with her — "I have lain by thee on the brown forest floor/ Beside thee, my Lady" — and praises her. All nature pays its homage — the watery freshets like peasants: "They jostle white-armed down the tent-bordered/ thoroughfare." The poem is rather stilted in its language and in its medieval homage to a Lady, but the theme of woman as nature's source of life, of whom he has taken possession, lies at the center of the poem. It anticipates *In the American Grain* (1925) in its theme of possession: "Of the pursuit of beauty and the husk that remains, perversions and mistakes, while the true form escapes in the wind, sing O Muse; of Raleigh, beloved by majesty, plunging his lust into the body of a new world — ."[5] Raleigh's conquest of the land was followed by "deaths, misfortunes,.. defeat," a theme that Williams would reiterate in *In the American*

Grain; but in "First Praise," the union of the poet and the life-force in nature is uplifting and fruitful.

In another brief tribute to a virginal ideal, "Homage," praise is given to the first of many named and unnamed girls to follow: here Elvira in love is encapsuled in a "clear radiance," raised above the commonplace. Williams pursues a theme that will recur in later poems: the transforming quality of love for even the humblest people. But love is a by-path, not a great highway, suggesting perhaps secretiveness, something difficult to find, often stolen. The praise implied in the title is consistent with all the early poems; the source is always love, which makes her radiance a supernal quality surpassing the gratuitous light of candles at noon.

"The Birth of Venus" and "Con Brio" both celebrate the salubriousness of physical love and scoff at the contemporary notion that sexual play should be a forbidden pleasure. Venus of course suggests the duality: the birth of love and the dangers of love. In this brief song, the mermaids, Circelike, invite the poet to join in their play. Familiar images of keen eyes and bright hair and stately form lure the poet to the "forbidden" pleasure. The siren call holds the promise of freedom, fulfillment, creativity, and the joy of tasting the forbidden fruit. Water as life will recur again in *Paterson*, but even before then, in "The Wanderer," when the female spirit of the river tempts the poet to leap into the "filthy Passaic."

"Con Brio" is an argument against those who would view Lancelot's love for Guinevere as "sin." In his defense, the poet plays on the *carpe diem* argument that to hold back on life is to not live at all. To love is to "spend the gold." Acceptance *is* life; rejection is death—to be "miserly." Miserly is the way to describe Lancelot's detractors; such men have a "sick historical sight" if they think Lancelot repented of his "deed with Guinevere." Such reasoning would have us deny the fruits of the earth—deny the apple for its blossoms. Unnatural, if not unseemly to repudiate such harvest! Fear holds men back from pleasure, but not Lancelot:

> Lancelot, thought little, spent his gold and rode to fight
> Mounted, if God was willing, on a good steed.

The poem is light as its title suggests: "With Spirit." The argument is sprightly and plays upon spending gold (an erotic reference to copulation), upon the "bellied" fullness of the paradisal apples, upon the "waste" of innocence untried, and finally upon the phallic overtones of Lancelot "mounted" ("if God was willing") suggesting divine complicity. "Con Brio" is a delightful defense of adultery committed without a guilty conscience.

Although the three poems "To Mark Antony in Heaven," "Revelation," and "Portrait of a Lady" did not appear in the original publication of *The Tempers*, they clearly share the spirit, theme, and form of Williams' concerns and his approach to women during these early years and were written about the same time. "Mark Antony" evokes the Cleopatra theme of temptation, and as in his defense of Lancelot, the poet attempts to understand, if not justify, Antony's "cowardly" deed of retreat. It is significant that the poet assumes Antony has made it into Heaven, with God's forgiveness of his act. The poem begins with the reflective voice of the speaker—a lover perhaps himself—speculating on Antony's reasons for the tragic flight. He asks the question: "Why did you follow/ that beloved body/ with your ships at Actium?" The answer is implied in the question, in the reference to the "beloved body," for well Antony knew both the woman and the goddess.

> you saw her
> above the battle's fury—
> clouds and trees and grass—

Clearly, Cleopatra becomes, like Enobarbus' description of her in Shakespeare's play, more than a mere woman. She is all nature, all spirit: "clouds and trees and grass"—the symbol of the creative principle. Antony sought life, not death, and thus wins Heaven. Williams returns to his familiar image of woman as fertility goddess in whom all opposites are harmonized, all opposition stilled. In his own north room, the morning light has illumined "grass and clouds and trees" and he too achieves the sublime moment of stasis after love. Then he is one with Antony and all lovers who have escaped the "battle's fury."

In "The Revelation," a title that hints at more than the poem appears to reveal, the poet brings together reality and dream. In his dream, the speaker has been tempted by a girl "reaching out to me—." He knows the girl in life, but fantasy and reality blur in his mind when he recalls that she "leaned on the door of my car/ And stroked my hand—." The syntax is clear; the embrace belongs to the dream, but the girl belongs to reality. As the poem ends, we find the poet wrapped in a daytime fantasy no less pleasing:

> I shall pass her on the street
> We shall say trivial things
> To each other
> But I shall never cease
> To search her eyes
> For that quiet look—

And the "revelation"? Perhaps it is that all men seek to fulfill their dreams in fantasies-turned-real. The experience is surely commonplace, but the poet's "search" for communication will persist. The stubbornness of dreams emanates perhaps from the joy of remembered pleasure: "I awoke happy." And the need to penetrate the trivia of life for something more radiant was a lifelong quest for Williams—to find the "Beautiful Thing" in everyday experience.

"Portrait of a Lady," partly tongue in cheek, affirms one source of fulfillment: the sensuous pleasure afforded by the female body. But it is more. For the subject has been raised to the level of art—here, in the paintings of Fragonard and Watteau. The poem, like the paintings, combines sexuality and plenitude. The woman *is* the appletree, the southern breeze, a gust of snow, the tall grass and the shore whose "sand clings to my lips." She is crystalline nature, but she is also sensual temptation, and she draws him to her as she herself lured the painter. The Lady in "Portrait" is both Virgin and Whore, richly voluptuous yet as enigmatic and mysterious and untouchable as the shore the poet fails to define. In the artist's painting, all opposites are fused: the real and the fanciful, the virginal and the erotic. Williams offers us an image of the female principle, fusing all disparities in his portrait in the final lines. "I said petals from an appletree." We are returned to the first humorous exaggeration of the woman: "Your thighs are appletrees/ whose blossoms touch the sky." Sensual and spiritual conjoin in an image of the "Beautiful Thing": "I said petals from an appletree."

In each of the poems I have glanced at briefly from this early volume, particular images of women with their multiple associations had already become formulated in Williams' imagination. Notably, the erotic—the Circe quality of each girl or woman—emerges in the poems. His own amorous experiences evoke Venus or Cleopatra or Guinevere or the lush beauties of Fragonard and Watteau. They are young Eves whose beauty tempts man to "experience," and that experience is both marvelous and terrible. Frequently, the female conjures up the fecund quality of the natural world, thus taking on mythic proportions. But these are only "hints and guesses," and the short imagistic poems give us glimpses rather than sustained portraits. The tone is one of homage, admiration, celebration, and awe. No poem signals this more clearly than "The Shadow," written about 1914 and found in a letter to Viola Jordan.[6] Here, Spring, a Koreate figure, "so soft, so smooth, and so cool," entices the speaker into darkness. The second stanza offers an early instance of Williams' predilection to identify the lover with nature; it is she who embraces him:

> Spring closes me in
> with her blossomy hair
> brings dark to my eyes.

Like the poems of this period, the mystery, the sensuousness, the suggestion of life and death in love are intoxicating temptations to which the poet willingly yields. Persephone as both virgin and whore is hinted at, closing in on him in a total experience of light and of darkness.

"The Wanderer"

Written in 1914, "The Wanderer" appears to be the seminal poem not only for *Paterson* but for many of Williams' themes and images that accrued in meaning in his later work. This is true especially in his use of the Demeter figure modeled on his grandmother, Emily Wellcome. The early hints of the "female principle" have already been noted in the brief poems before 1914. Williams himself, in an interview, said that "The Wanderer" was indeed the genesis of Paterson, inspired by his grandmother. It started, he said

> as the idealization of my grandmother, Mrs. Wellcome.... The figure of my grandmother in "The Wanderer" was semi-mythical.... In "The Wanderer" I identified my grandmother with my poetic un-conscious. She was the personification of poetry. I wanted to identify myself with something good and philosophical — with a perfect knowledge of the world. I thought of myself as all-good and all-wise. So the grandmother who was the spirit of the river, led to the Passaic. "The Wanderer" was a disappointed, a defeated person — myself. Then came *Paterson*, a greater realization of immediate surroundings.[7]

In this brief summary, Williams easily equated the woman, the creative im-agination, and the poem. He would reiterate this union many times in his later poetry.

One would think that Williams' own explication of the poem would suffice, but critics have focused repeatedly on this early poem because of its relation to *Paterson*. I should like to note only those aspects of "The Wanderer" that suggest Williams' development of the Kore/Demeter theme, one that demonstrates his continuing interest in the duality of women, and reveals the beginnings of his notion of the virgin/whore. In addition, I invite the readers of this poem to note a peculiar reversal in "The Wanderer" in which the *male poet* is the innocent Kore figure, wandering in search of union with a life-giving activity. Williams' gloss on the Kore/Demeter myth unites, therefore, two aspects of the myth: the innocence of Kore and the wandering of Demeter.

The poem we know is an admixture of fact and fantasy. Crossing the ferry to Manhattan, confused and weary in an identity crisis of his own, the innocent wanderer-poet undergoes, through a mystical experience, a ritual of death and rebirth. But not before he has received his "education" from the tutelary spirit of the river. Most of the poem deals with his novitiate. The situation evokes the divine Demeter's revelations of the mysteries of Eleusis to the young princes.

We are introduced to the river spirit in "Advent" where, as a young crow, she invites the young wanderer to soar with her above the horizon, beyond the reaches of the woods, beyond reality into that other realm that is the imagination: "I know now how then she showed me/ Her mind ..."

He has yet to see her in her true form, but once on the river he glimpses her fleetingly in a vision while he wrestles with his problem of becoming a poet in the modern world. He follows her in his mind, yielding to her invitation to "play," acknowledging her as his tutelary spirit. "For me one face is all the world!/ For I have seen her at last, this day,/ In whom age in age is united — ." In this part of the poem ("Clarity"), the river spirit is revealer, creator, goddess — but old. All the associations of Demeter are here: the disguised old crone, the universal mother, the wanderer, the key to the mysteries of the life-force, the nourisher of the mind, without whom the poet cannot free himself from the lethargy that overcomes him. She is indeed

> That high wanderer of by-ways
> Walking imperious in beggary!

The motif of Wisdom disguised as the whore will recur in Williams' poetry as late as "The Desert Music," in which the old whore in the dance hall still has something to teach him. The crone here takes shape before him — reduced by age, "diminished," but still grand and demanding. She is power, feigning powerlessness, and in "Broadway" she becomes the gull as she reveals to him the tragedy of the city streets. In an awful moment, he sees her in yet another form — as the old whore, leading him perhaps to death and destruction. Clearly a symbol of reality, the disguised female spirit is as sullied and repugnant as the tawdry city she unfolds. At first he recoils:

> ... And then for the first time
> I really saw her, really scented the sweat
> Of her presence and — fell back sickened!
> Ominous, old, painted —

The images are, at first repulsive: she is lewd and painted, old, yet willing herself to be young. Humbling himself before her, he entreats the "marvelous old Queen" to give him power to serve her. She *is* the whore who bespeaks the experience of lust; she *is* the crafty prowler; she *is* the purveyor of knowledge who, like Demeter, can give him life or death. Here for the first time in an important poem, Williams commits himself to the value of experience: lewd or tattered though its disguise may be in the real world, the "radiant gist" lies submerged beneath the filth and banality. He implores the old crone ("The Strike"): "Great Queen, bless me with thy tatters!" The poet is now the novitiate, a Kore figure wandering the deserted streets of a hellish modern world. What he discovers is the violation of innocence, a theme he will expand upon in "To Elsie." "Everywhere the electric!" he observes. The young whores are ruined virgins with "sagging breasts and protruding stomachs." He sees spiritual death everywhere and is endangered himself until the river spirit sweeps him up in "Abroad," where he repays her with the promise to be her "voice." "Speak to men of these, concerning me!" The world will not hear her except through his voice — an instrument yet unequal to the task. She gives his voice power by making him old. He becomes strong, mighty, an Atlas among men: part human, part divine. She invites him to enjoy his newfound power to harmonize all evil and all good.

In the final section of "The Wanderer" ("St. James Grove"), the poet experiences his death and rebirth in a ritual of immersion: ". . . the novitiate was ended/ . . . the life begun." He follows the old crone to the Passaic. There she invokes the river god to accept the wanderer's soul. The experience is climactic as she urges him:

> "Enter, youth, into this bulk!
> Enter, river, into this young man!"
> Then the river began to enter my heart,
> . . . .
> And I knew all — it became me.

In a significant metaphor that haunted Williams throughout his life, the leap into the river is a coalescence of fear and hope, death and rebirth in the muddy waters, the crystal beauty of the swift-running river, the degradation and the uplifting into a new tide, a new life. He becomes the river and the river becomes him.

"The Wanderer" concludes with the emergence of the river goddess in all her grandeur, mate of the river god, who has given her "son" a new life. For this "gift" she promises the god a "bird's paradise," an eternity to the river. For the poet, the new wanderer, she leaves remembrance of her self and her sorrow. Of these he will speak, for now he knows what she knows. The trial by immersion recalls the experience of Demaphoon, the child plunged into the fire by Demeter. Here snatched back to life by his tutelary spirit, the poet returns, new-made, his destiny — to wander — awaiting him. And, indeed, Mr. Paterson is the "wanderer" of Williams' American myth, plunging into the "filthy Passaic" again and again.

The female spirit in "The Wanderer," though inspired, as Williams declared, by his grandmother, Emily Wellcome, owes much to the figure of Demeter, as I have shown (Chapter II). The poet himself evokes the Kore maiden: innocent, initiated by violence and degradation, but always returned to life and springtime: "backward and forward." Crucial in the poem is the union in the female spirit of all opposites: "In whom age in age is united." He will immortalize her in "The Wanderer" even as he aimlessly wanders the urban waste, searching for its past and its truth. Like Whitman before him, he will be the "arbiter of the diverse," and he will bring forth both the "filthy Passaic" and the Beautiful Thing. The old crone, both virgin and whore — "Good is my over lip and evil/ My under lip to you henceforth:/ For I have taken your soul between my two hands/ And this shall be as it is spoken" — will bring together all of his worlds: the world of Paterson, the world of the creative spirit, the world of art — the poem.

Throughout the early poems, as I shall demonstrate, this thematic thread is woven into the very fabric of Williams' poetry: the theme of woman as a life force signaling both death and rebirth of the land and man's inexorable link with that cycle. The "Kore motif" is thus developed not only in "The Wanderer" but in poems that appear in *Al Que Quiere!* (1917) and *Spring and All* (1923); it is central to *Paterson* and continues to haunt Williams' old age in *Pictures from Brueghel*. Several poems complement "The Wanderer" and demonstrate the growth of this important and consistent idea in Williams' poetry.

"Immortal" is an early poem in this genre and touches subtly on the Demeter/Kore myth. The address is to the loved one, "Ignorance," . . . whose qualities belie her name and invite us to substitute "Innocence." She is "braver than all flowers,/ richer than clear gems; wider than the sky;/ Immortal and unchangeable; whose powers/ Transcend reason, love, and sanity!" Suggested here is the Kore maiden in all her initial purity, but also suggested in the poem is the Demeter figure "marvelous and terrible." She is an injured Juno, "roused against Heaven's King!" evoking Demeter's fiery wrath against Zeus. The despoiled Demeter, and the violated Kore by extension (her "ignorance" made her prey to Hades' betrayal of her innocence), conjure up the duality of the virgin and the whore. Only the goddess can reconcile the opposites posed in the poem. And who *is* "thou, beloved" to whom the poet raises his voice in tribute, equating her with all that is immortal in woman? The riddle lies, but it is sufficient that she is "that godly thing"—in innocence or ignorance, sharing with the wronged Juno a righteous wrath and power. "Immortal" is one of Williams' early imagistic experiments. The juxtaposition of images recalls Pound's dictum: "An Image is that which presents an intellectual and emotional complex in an instant of time."[8] And in Williams' poem, the lover is, for a moment in time, one with flower, gems, sky, and injured Juno, intimating an equation of "unexpected exactness."[9]

Although "January Morning" (see Chapter II) does not introduce a particular woman as the centerpiece of the poem, it is memorable on several counts. First, the poem is dedicated to Emily Wellcome:

> All this—
>   was for you, old woman.
> I wanted to write a poem
> that you would understand.

"January Morning" is Williams as Kore, awakening from the darkness of lifeless winter to the hints of emerging spring. The poet is on a ferry—the real world of Dr. Williams on his way to the hospital. As if anticipating the river spirit in "The Wanderer" in her youth, his own "spirit is/ a white gull with delicate pink feet." He is happy, dancing, for though the signs of winter are all around him, he senses the rebirth of the land. "January Morning" is a "new" poem for Williams in some respects. It is longer than the poems in the earlier volumes with the exception of "The Wanderer," but the collage technique is closer to the poetry he will write later. The connective tissue is submerged, and the poem rests upon the juxtaposition of images of death and life. Life triumphs against winter darkness as the sun suffuses the scene, and the tension of the poem depends subtly on our sense of the poet's identification with the rite of spring. He dances.

In a lesser-known poem, "Spring Strains," *(Al Que Quiere!)* the poet begins with the monotones always associated with winter: blues and greys, here joined in the blue-grey buds, the blue-grey twigs, the blue-grey birds. But suddenly, the signs of new life struggle to appear:

> the blinding and red-edged sun-blur—
> creeping energy, concentrated
> counterforce—welds sky, buds, trees,
> rivets them in one puckering hold!
> Sticks through! Pulls the whole
> counter-pulling mass upward . . .

Spring, the "creeping energy" promises unity and wholeness, coherence and order after the death of disorderly winter. "Spring Strains" suggests the difficulty of the emergent birth, and in "Spring and All" Williams emphasizes the laboriousness of bringing life out of nothingness. Although a woman does not appear in these poems, spring is clearly a female force, and the pangs of labor suggest parturition.

In "Spring and All" everything appears to be lifeless, "By the road to the contagious hospital." But the sensitive listener knows that ". . . sluggish/ dazed spring approaches—," like the newborn children Williams had ushered into the world:

> They enter the new world naked,
> cold, uncertain of all
> save that they enter.

"Spring and All" is Kore's return, both a source of joy and a source of pathos. Order is restored, for the land will be fruitful again: "One by one objects are defined—." In the last lines, the earth has undergone its metamorphosis from death to life:

> . . . Still, the profound change
> has come upon them: rooted, they
> grip down and begin to awaken

Williams associates his own awakening senses with the return of the life force. "I am Kora," he was fond of saying through much of his life.

In 1930, he had published in the *Imagiste Anthology* a long poem dedicated to the return of spring: "Della Primavera Transportata Al Morale." The poem opens in April—the "beginning"—with another reference to a Koreate figure: "the dress/ in which the veritable winter/ walks in Spring—." The hymn to spring is interrupted by the insistent incursion of fragments from the prosaic world: the buying and selling of property, deformity, the clatter of life on the city streets with its concrete mixers, its shining river mud, its howling wind. Amid all this, spring enters, and with it love, though man knows only starvation of the spirit: ". . . April is a thing/ comes just the same—" After mockingly cataloguing all the modern "beliefs"— in country, law enforcement, tariffs, "in giving the farmer and/ land owner adequate protection"—the poet returns to the only belief he holds: love.

The rest of the poem reiterates his conviction that the city inhabitants are "lost." "Winter: Spring/ abandoned in you. The world lost—/ in you." This will become a central motif in *Paterson*. And spring enters unnoticed (much as it does in "Spring and All") amid the realities of the sprawling urban wasteland. All remains wintry and fierce and barren.

The coming of spring, Williams asserts in several poems, is likened to human birth: hard and bitter and often without the joy of recognition. But life, as "Full Moon" testifies, does return if one responds with love in "the warm/ the radiant/ all fulfilling/ day."

It is this rebirth he will seek in *Paterson*. As early as 1927, the "idea" of Paterson had taken possession of him and, interestingly, the short poem "Paterson" begins in the depths of winter, "Before the grass is out the people are out/ and bare twigs still whip the wind—/ when there is nothing in the pause between/ snow and grass in the parks and at the street ends." The deadness of winter and snow cover Paterson as the poet moves out into his world searching for love and spring.

By 1940, in "Paterson: Episode 17," the poet had already begun the myth he would construct as a larger work. The season here is summer, but the "Beautiful Thing" has already been violated, degraded, betrayed, and the speaker despairs:

> till I must believe that all
> desired women have had each
> in the end
> a busted nose
> and live afterward marked up
> Beautiful Thing

Since Williams incorporated most of this passage in *Paterson*, I will consider it in its larger context, but it is worth noting here that the two Paterson poems serve as a thematic bridge between "The Wanderer" and the larger myth, for-mulating many of the themes already hinted in the earlier shorter poems. The ephemeral images of love, the barrenness of modern man, the violation

of beauty in the emblem of Kore — all provide a counterpart for Williams'
emotions of despair or joy, hope, or pity.

The poems in *Al Que Quiere!* are largely brief, impressionistic snapshots — often local, often personal, often reflections on the passing scene, or
songs and celebrations of Emily Wellcome, still very much a part of
Williams' consciousness. The virtues he extols are her strength, determination, self-sufficiency — even though an alien and a wanderer — and her gift for
survival. I have already mentioned Williams' autobiographical tribute to
Emily, "Dedication to a Plot of Ground" (Chapter III). Her power and endurance in a strange land evokes his admiration, as well as his contempt for
those of weaker stuff. Emily is a "living presence." To the rest, he would
warn, "If you can bring nothing to this place,/ but your carcass, keep
out!"

Emily's strength is also recognized in the egg woman walking the streets
of Rutherford, a ". . . powerful woman,/ coming with swinging haunches,
breasts straight forward/ supple shoulders, full arms/ and strong, soft hands
(I've felt them)/ carrying a heavy basket." From the dead land she is an image
of life coming toward him, and he exults at the sight of her:

> You walking out toward me
> from that dead hillside.

Her "grey eyes" and her "kind mouth" transform the commonplace encounter
into a momentary communion.

In several poems about women in this volume, as well as in earlier
poems, the poet's contact is made through the eyes of the woman. The eyes,
sometimes "keen," sometimes "kind grey eyes," communicate when one cannot speak, but the eyes "perceive" the truth beneath the surface of ordinary
reality. In "Portrait of a Woman in Bed," the old whore, Robitza, can still
say, "But I've my two eyes/ and a smooth face." In "Virtue," the vulgarity
of the whore is redeemed by her eyes, "the smile of her." Once again,
Williams brings together the crudeness and the compensating loveliness of
woman. The whore on the street is neither new, nor lasting, nor terribly interesting, save for the eyes that understand the futility of life, the emptiness
that Williams so often sensed within himself. What the eye sees, Williams
would emphasize in all his poetry, is the only truth to be captured. In "The
Red Wheelbarrow," "so much depends" on the perception of the poet — and
the reader — as each arranges the bits and fragments of commonplace objects. The artist transforms them into a work of beauty — a painting, a poem,
something that endures. Here in the poem, the whore's virtue is her
knowledge of the "emptiness" that increases the urgency of her call to all men
to enjoy her "gifts": "old men with dirty beards,/ men in vests with/ gold
watch chains. Come!" The siren call is most strong in the image of experience. It is not the virgin who tempts but the whore. It is again the

tattered old crone who catches his eye as he wanders the urban streets, an odd commingling of "fatted bosoms" and chrysanthemums, of vulgarity and beauty coexisting in a single image. The poet notes in "Smell!": ". . . With what deep thirst/ we quicken our desires/ to that rank odor of a passing springtime!. . . Must you taste everything? Must you know everything?/ Must you have a part in everything?" Clearly, the answer is "Yes!" Another poem, "Canthara" testifies to the relentlessness of reconsidered passion. Even the old man recalls the dancing naked women: "their breasts:/ bellies flung forward/ knees flying!" and in the dingy bathroom he "swished with ecstasy to/ the familiar music of/ his old emotion."

But the lusty whore is not the only image of temptation. Often, the temptress is young and refreshingly unconscious of her beauty. In a memorable poem, Williams catches a glimpse of a young housewife through his car window, and the moment brings an interval of pleasure and, again, communion. Here is "The Young Housewife" one could have seen on countless New Jersey streets, but Williams' portrait transmutes her into an urban Venus: vulnerable, ephemeral, both innocent and seductive in the caught moment. Driving up and down the streets of Rutherford, he glimpses for one moment an object of beauty; his response is to drive by, solitary in his car, smiling and bowing his pleasure.

> At ten A.M. the young housewife
> moves about in negligee behind
> the wooden walls of her husband's house.
> . . . .
> shy, uncorseted, tucking in
> stray ends of hair, and I compare her
> to a fallen leaf.

The moment of pathos goes by almost unnoticed as he compares her to a "fallen leaf," a theme that will continue to haunt him in later poetry: the ephemeral quality of innocence, still redolent of a lost Eden. But the theme of "experience" compels him even more. He wrote in *Kora*:

> In France, the country of Rabelais, they know that the world is
> not made up entirely of virgins. They do not deny virtue to the rest
> because of that. Each age has its perfections but the praise differs. . . .
> Their girls, also, thrive upon the love-making they get, so much so that
> the world runs to Paris for that reason.[10]

On the one hand, the passage is an amusing defense of the "virtue" of love-making as opposed to virginity; on the other, it is a recognition of the value of "experience" for Williams would always associate a knowledge of the world with the knowledge of love. Sometimes, that wisdom could only by gleaned by a periodic leap into the filthy Passaic. Women always have something to sell me, he reiterated much of his life, and the theme of seeking such

knowledge is persistent in the poetry. In "The Waitress," Williams begins
again with the magic of the woman's eyes:

> No wit (and none needed) but
> the silence of her ways, grey eyes in
> a depth of black lashes —
> The eyes look and the look falls.

Here is another "victim" of the modern city: the roughened hands, the
broken knuckles, the stained wrist. Yet he can say to her, "All the rest are
liars, all but you." The "waitress" carries the double entendre of "waiting
upon" the men — serving the food in the cheap diner or waiting upon their
desires. The figure is a symphony of sexual allure " — and the movements/
under the scant dress . . ." stir the senses. But she is aloof though nothing
in the city is alive but her.

> Wait on us, wait
> on us with your momentary beauty to be enjoyed by
> none of us. Neither by you, certainly,
> nor by me.

Like the "Beautiful Thing" in *Paterson*, she is just beyond his reach, and the
momentary beauty is "enjoyed by/ none of us."

Williams warns us in the foreword to his autobiography that he does not
"intend to tell the particulars of the women I have been to bed with, or
anything about them. Don't look for it." He goes on to say, nonetheless, "I
am extremely sexual in my desires: I carry them everywhere and at all
times."[11] The passage is amusing because one does not need from Williams
a catalog of his sexual exploits — however much that might titillate the public
fancy! But the poems themselves, often remarkably frank and precise, tell
us more about this "Don Juan in a Model-T" than any gratuitous
autobiographical "confessions."

We have only to look at several of the poems in *Sour Grapes*, the most
personal of all Williams' early volumes, to sense the depth of his awareness
of women, both as sexual objects and as symbols of a life force he found ir-
resistible. With a single exception, the speaker is always "I." In "The Gentle
Man," we are privy to the personal yet universal experience of recollected
passion:

> I feel the caress of my own fingers
> on my own neck as I place my collar
> and think pityingly
> of the kind women I have known.

"Arrival" is the account of a tryst, but the poem is saved from mere confession by the sensitivity of the lover who equates the "tawdry body" with the

dying emblems of nature in autumn: the "silk and linen leaves," the winter wind heralding death and desolation. "Arrival" is an admixture of reality and fantasy and the central image one of delicacy and beauty:

> And yet one arrives somehow,
> . . . .
> feels the autumn
> dropping its silk and linen leaves
> about her ankles.

The poem ends with an exclamation, as though the poet is surprised to find an object of beauty in a tawdry and "strange" setting.

But the humorous side of Williams' dealings with women is reflected throughout the poetry as well: in his inclusion of Marcia Nardi's letters which revealed her tenacity in clinging to Williams for support; in his "Portrait of a Lady" which is not so much a parody of Eliot and Pound or James as it is his own sexual awareness of well-endowed females even in paintings such as Fragonard's. When queried about "Portrait," Williams laughed with Edith Heal "and agreed that it could not possibly have been suggested by the work" of either James or Eliot. Williams' hilarious account of the baroness' hot pursuit of him to Ridge Avenue is as much a jibe at his own faculty for "women trouble" as it is a ridicule of the baroness, whom he helped later when she was in desperate financial straits. Finally, his amusing poem "Exercise No. 2" takes note of what happens in old age as he greets his neighbor:

> an old lady as I am an old man
> we greet each other
>
> across the hedge
> my wife gives her flowers
> we have never visited each other

Yet in a nostalgic moment, all his affection for women comes rushing back as in "15 Years Later" he returns to an old theme: the completion of man by woman. The poem is autobiographic in nature: he is the playwright and the doctor with his patients, and the way that the two parts of his life come together in art — here in the play *Many Loves*.

Two poems that are revealing for their autobiographical "frankness" are "The Jungle" and "Rain." The first is a thumbnail sketch of all the turmoil, danger, and chaos equated with a casual visit to a whorehouse. The jungle is not the conventional wilderness of the natural world, but the wilderness of the spirit that leads the speaker to his destination. The syntax of the poem is stark: the jungle is not the woods

                              but —
                a girl waiting
                shy, brown, soft-eyed —
                to guide you
                              Upstairs, sir.

In "Rain," a longer poem already noted, Williams justifies illicit love as
an erotic experience valued in its own right, as a means of cleansing the soul,
as an integral part of nature's own means of bathing. Life arises anew from
the rain that "falls upon the earth/ and grass and flowers," which achieve
perfection from such nourishment. Here, as in so many poems in this period
of his life, Williams warmly asserts that woman is the center, the essence of
goodness in the world, and he enthusiastically searches for her to complete
himself. The "rain" of love is a physician itself — healing, resurrecting, but
in truth not changing the world. The poem ends with an understate-
ment, but with an ironic twist reaffirms the *power* of love to save the
world:

                But love is
                unworldly
                        and nothing
                comes of it but love
                following
                and falling endlessly
                from
                        her thoughts

It would be too narrow a vision to see "Rain" as simply Williams' attempt to justify illicit love, though it is illicit love that begins the poem. More
importantly, he is arguing for the same proposition so succinctly put by
Frost: "Earth's the right place for love:/ I don't know where it's likely to go
better." The conviction that men must touch that "radiant gist" through an
experience of communication, human communion, is a kind of religion to
Williams who had no formal religious answer for the sadness and waste of
modern life.

"To a Friend Concerning Several Ladies" is another poem suggestive of
more complicated themes than mere sexual temptation. The erotic is present, but beyond that, the importance of women to the creative imagination.
The "women" will make a man of him, and he will "with love on his shoulder"
create the poem that waits to be written. The poet moves through several
stages. He *would* be happy with the innocent things of nature, a ". . . few
chrysanthemums/ half lying on the grass," or ". . . the/ talk of a few people,
the trees,/ an expanse of dried leaves," but the siren call beckons him,
perhaps in the message of the eyes, ". . . a look — well-placed," and then he
is confused, twisted, left flat. If he does not submit, he becomes stale and the
poem will not be written, and so he heeds the call:

> ... There is
> no good in the world except out of
> a woman and certain women alone
> for certain things.

Innumerable times, here and elsewhere, Williams offers the paradox of the forbidden fruit and the creative stimulus: the whore and the virgin who combine to produce "the good in the world." The need to complete himself both as a man and as a poet through love is a theme that figures largely in these early poems.

Williams' attitudes were, as I have suggested earlier, shaped by the women patients to whom he was called often in the middle of the night or in the frozen wintry waste. "They call me and I go," he says in "Complaint," and despite the snowy and dangerous trip, he enters smiling. Here is life in the middle of death, but not entering with beauty and subtlety. It is life torn out of the vomiting woman on the bed:

> I pick the hair from her eyes
> and watch her misery
> with compassion.

On another cold night, he is obsessed by ". . . the bare thighs of/ the Police Sergeant's wife — among/ her five children . . ." In the depth of winter, he dreams about the springtime — April — when he will see her again:

> The round and perfect thighs
> of the Police Sergeant's wife
> perfect still after many babies.
> Oya!

Clearly, his intimate knowledge of the Police Sergeant's wife came during the delivery of the five babies, but that does not prevent the dreamer in the night from relishing the image of beauty in a winter fantasy as he yearns for April and perfect beauty. Always, when "desolate" or lonely, or weighed down by thoughts of winter and death — so that he sees himself as Kora — the thought of woman uplifts and saves him. "The Desolate Field" expresses this experience with delicacy and insight:

> . . . amazed my heart leaps
> at the thought of love
> vast and grey
> yearning silently over me.

Happiness was not always a stolen pleasure, a by-path in the night. Williams experiences moments of deep and abiding pleasure in the safe and familiar emblems of home: Flossie's slippers, the plums he steals from the refrigerator at night, the order and coherence of a life that is often in inner turmoil and restlessness. But these moments of quiet happiness were not common when Williams was young and alternately angry or despairing or weighted down by an oppressive sense of loneliness. The need to find the life force, to search for the return of springtime to cover that solitude, is movingly reflected in the poem "Blizzard." It begins with the snow that "drifts its weight/ deeper and deeper for three days/ or sixty years, eh?" At the close of the poem, we have a glimpse of the inner man, Elena's alien son:

> The man turns and there —
> his solitary tracks stretched out
> upon the world.

He had said early, "I am a pessimist and I must lift myself by my bootstraps," but in this intimate moment we share his existential loneliness and his keen awareness of the need for the sun and the return of spring after winter's blizzard.

We recall that in "The Wanderer" the disguised goddess instructs the young poet to speak for her: "Speak to men of these . . ." In the poems that appeared between 1923 (with the publication of *Spring and All*) and 1938, Williams kept his pledge to the river spirit. He had called out in "The Wanderer": "Waken! my people, to the boughs green/ With ripening fruit within you!/ Waken to the myriad cinquefoil/ In the waving grass of your minds!" But as he hurries ". . . shivering/ Out in the deserted streets of Paterson," he discovers a far more tarnished world and a people unable to recover that primitive purity, that "ripening fruit" within, to which he had urged them to awaken.

Instead, the poems that emerge reflect his observation of tragedy and violation and lost innocence. The significant poem of this group is "To Elsie," which opens with the prophetic line: "The pure products of America go crazy." Elsie is the hired girl in every doctor's house, the whored virgin, the violated Kore. I have noted elsewhere that the poem owes much to the myth of Demeter/Kore as Williams transmuted Kore's fate into the tragedy of the city slattern. I should like to add here that the theme of "whored innocence" also becomes a emblem for the betrayal of American ideals and hopes and dreams. The figure betrayed in Williams is always a woman who is a living testament of our failures. Significantly, the defiant imagination "strains/ after deer/ going by fields of goldenrod in/ the stifling heat of September." The aspiration is balanced in Williams' poem by the degradation. Though the poem concludes with an image of indirection, it is important to note that the lines before become the central thematic thread of *Paterson*:

> It is only in isolate flecks that
> something
> is given off.

Enigmatic, surely, but the "isolate flecks" seem always to save the poet in his deepest despair. Other poems that are snapshots of Elsie's world appear as companion pieces in *Spring and All* and other volumes after 1923: "The Deceptrices" dress like "whores" but are merely uncertain of their identity and "put on the bold/ looks of experience." "The Raper from Passenack" is a small drama of "some Elsie" raped and given a venereal disease: "What a mess she was in." Only death can save her, and she waits and wishes for it. But death is not always possible, and others also wait for the relief that does not come. Like the Cumaean Sibyl, the sick old patient of "To an Old Jaundiced Woman" longs for death, moaning in pain; the doctor beside her is impotent to save her either by life or death. Another victim in the modern city is the mother whose baby is dead, but who cannot die herself: "The mother's eyes where she sits/ by the window, unconsoled — / have purple bags under them." Tragedy is everywhere he looks; the "Young Woman at a Window" is another snapshot of despair: "She sits with/ tears on/ her cheek." As in many of Williams' imagistic poems, the woman becomes the equation of hopelessness, loneliness, and sorrow without the promise of expiation in the modern world of Paterson.

But not all the female portraits mirror the Elsies of his world; often he returns to his admiration of the strong women like his grandmother, with her power and endurance. In "Proletarian Portrait," he sees "A big young bareheaded woman/ in an apron/ Her hair slicked back standing/ on the street." She is young, strong, and Williams admires her. Similarly, the old woman enjoying her plums is a delightful portrait of woman and fruitfulness brought together in a single image:

> munching a plum on
> the street a paper bag
> of them in her hand

A "solace of ripe plums" becomes the occasion for a poem, a moment of contentment in an otherwise dull and meaningless world.

Elena Hoheb Williams appears early as the inspiration for several of Williams' poems of recollection, alienation, and the loneliness of old age with its scant resources for life. In "All the Fancy Things," he calls up the picture of the young, gifted girl, now old and unfulfilled, betrayed by life in which the present fails to measure up to the past:

> So that now
> she doesn't know what to do
>
> with herself alone
> and growing old up here —

An interesting gloss on this poem, with its lesson to "ma chère" to withstand the "rebuffs," is Williams' comment on Elena in *Kora*:

> She has always been incapable of learning from benefit or
> disaster. If a man cheat her she will remember that man with a violence
> that I have seldom equaled, but so far as that could have an influence
> on her judgment of the next man or woman, she must be living in
> Eden. And indeed she is, an impoverished, ravished Eden but one in-
> destructible as the imagination itself. Whatever is before her is suf-
> ficient to itself and so to be valued.[12]

In a longer poem (continuing the Eden theme), "Eve," the son humbles
himself before the aging woman, and chides her again for her stubborn battle
with time, admiring, all along, her strength and her "unappeased shame."
The poem begins with a request for forgiveness: "Pardon my injuries/ now
that you are old —" and he analyzes the old Elena even as she analyzes him,
the son. She pities him, perhaps because as he says, she is ashamed to see
him as she does, paradoxically as he sees her: defenseless, without subtlety.
He acknowledges her desire "to escape and leap into chaos" with his own wish
to escape the barriers of time and place, yet helpless before their onslaught.
He would protect her as he would protect himself from reaching out "to self-
inflicted emptiness — ," and he would return life to her:

> I will write a book about you—
> making you live (in a book!)
> as you still desperately
> want to live —
> to live always — unforgiving

Williams of course (together with Elena) wrote the book *Yes, Mrs. Williams*,
and through his mother's recollections, relives those idyllic days in
Mayaguez, recapturing bits of her youth and for the moment defeating time.
Yes, Mrs. Williams was the poet's labor of love for the "wasted carcass" that
was once the aspiring, sensitive artist. It was a means as well to expiate his
own fears of age and death. He had never been close to her, he says in "Eve,"
but that was because "I am like you." "Eve" is only one of several poems
Williams wrote for Elena, but it reveals as much of his own fears and
powerlessness as it is a portrait of an old woman and death.

Poems: 1944-1950

> "It isn't masculine more than it is
> feminine. . ."
>
> "Writer's Prologue to a Play in Verse"

In the shorter poems written between 1944 and 1950, during which time
Williams had already begun his American myth, *Paterson*, many of the
themes and images that had preoccupied him earlier continued to emerge in

recurrent patterns. Briefly, Williams was still compelled by the women who peopled his everyday life, who would be models for the "innumerable women" of *Paterson*: Elena, Flossie, and the hundreds of nameless women, some patients, others merely strangers glimpsed from his car window. He continued to dwell on the erotic experience and the way "love" transcended all the sordidness of life as he observed it around him. Although Mike Weaver quotes Williams' declaration that "Love and beauty are eternally separate," — that is, the "Seductive and the Beautiful were not ... the same,"[13] the poetry is a living refutation of that assertion. Weaver believes the confusion arises when Williams equates "love" with "sex"; yet nowhere in his poetry does Williams make any meaningful distinction between the two. Sex and love are bound up inextricably because sex is related to the female principle of fecundity, and love and beauty have their sources in this life-giving surge. I would suggest that Williams' "intellectualizing" the point is weak evidence; the weight of conviction lies in countless poems in which the erotic experience often leads to a stasis of the spirit, creativity in the imagination, and a momentary escape from the inexorable dullness and tragedy in ordinary lives. In many ways, *Paterson* is a search for that magical element that could transmute reality.

Thus, the later short poems are also a collage of snapshots or "still" moments after lovemaking. Williams' fascination with the virgin and the whore led to many poems about this enigmatic aspect of women. He wrote, "Innocence! Innocence is the condition of heaven," as he observed more and more about him the vestiges of lost virginity. The whore, on the other hand, had her special charm. In a letter to Kenneth Burke in 1943, he jokingly recounted his smalltalk with the nurses:

> I was telling the girls on the obstetric floor this afternoon that when I get old I'm going to look for a job as houseman in a whorehouse. I'm still crazy about the women, I just like them around and having enjoyed them and given them some enjoyment I feel now that I have earned the right to be right in among them. No sexes barred — just the relaxing hell of it. Rabelais is my patron.[14]

The "whore" continued to accrue in meaning, not merely the worn-out trader in sexual favors (though she is always that in Rutherford's world), but the image for countless symbolic suggestions, all beginning with "The Wanderer." She is experience, wisdom, truth, freedom, the tutelary power of the experienced lover, the source of fecundity and renewal. As the virgin and the whore begin to come together in *Paterson*, the paradox is hinted at in several short poems: ideal and real, sacred and profane, ignorant and wise, death and life.

One group of poems, largely imagistic snapshots, captures the "innumerable women" of Rutherford: we see them, hear their voices, note their magical eyes, their power and their powerlessness. "What makes them tick?" he once asked. We hear her in "Catastrophic Birth":

> Shut up! laughs the big she-Wop.
> Wait till you have six like a me.
> Every year one. Come on! Push!

or in "A Cold Front," where we see the woman who has seven babies and wants an abortion. Yet clinging to the lifeless human wreck with expressionless eyes is a vestigial beauty:

> and there is a dull flush
> almost of beauty to the woman's face

In a less tragic moment, the ordinary woman in "A Woman in Front of a Bank" poses an image of beauty on the ugly city street: just a woman, baby in tow, who still carries an impudent eroticism that stops the poet to look upon her. The moment affords a refreshing bit of relief from the formality of the bank. Again, a moment of pleasure is captured in "The Girl" when he watches a girl "with big breasts/ under a blue sweater/ bareheaded —/ crossing the street" or the child in the empty lot playing ball in "Philomena Andronico," a capsule portrait of youthful grace. The child, all movement and life, is completely unconscious of her innocent charm, poised as if waiting for life to take over, perhaps to give someone pleasure like the eyes that watch her, perhaps to fall as the final lines imply.

In another group of poems, Williams returns to the theme now familiar in his poetry: the erotic experience heightened by a transcendent vision that fuses his twin worlds of reality and imagination. In "A Flowing River"—a love song—the poet compares his love to ". . . a river/ under tranquil skies —" where "the current moves/ to what sea that shines/ and ripples in my thought." The aftermath of love, always quiet, always "tranquil," escapes "imperfections" and leaves the lovers suffused in the image of the shining sea. In "Wide Awake, Full of Love," he less romantically reflects on the seduction: "What of your dish-eyes/ that have seduced/ me? Your voice/ whose cello notes/ upon the theme have led/ me to the music?" In a flash of truth, he sees her as she really is: scrawny, with thinning hair and worn thighs, but almost instantly he is drawn back "half ill with love."

Other poems also play on the theme of erotic love, sometimes with Williams' rare humor edged with irony: "You are a typical American woman/ you think men grow on trees —/ You want love, only love! rarest/ of male fruit! . . ." In "Chanson" he celebrates that sexuality: ". . . No counterfeit, no mere/ metal to be sure —/ yet, a treasury. . . ." But the woman is more than the ". . . riches/ of her sex . . .": "Her thoughts are to her/ like fruit to the tree, the apple, the pear./ She thinks and thinks well . . ." The world she creates surpasses all known worlds, and he would gladly remain there.

The pleasure in identifying with the female world is one Williams revealed in all his poetry; it becomes especially poignant in the last poems *Pictures from Brueghel* and in the last book of *Paterson*, when to recover himself he will recognize the "female principle" within himself. In "St. Valentine" he brings together male and female as a defense against the "cities rotted/ to pig sties":

> A woman's breasts
> for beauty
> A man's delights
> for charm

The combination, as he will argue in *Paterson*, is indestructible. "Let us praise! praise/ the dreadful symbol of/ carnivorous sex — / The gods live!" he wrote in "All That Is Perfect in Woman."

The most sustained poem on the theme of the transforming power of love is "A Crystal Maze." The lover is called upon to learn that love is to take possession: by giving, laying oneself bare, offering. In return he is offered love:

> Take it, black curls clustered in
> the hollow of the neck, unwilling
> to be released for less —
> laying desperately with impeccable
> composure an unnecessary
> body clean to the eye —

Touching then upon the transformation of love, Williams again refers to those emotions that always recur when he sees beauty in woman: amazement, the sea change, the humility. He goes on to accept love's supremacy over him:

> Loosed to take its course, love
> is the master —

The poem is about erotic love — the giving and the taking. It is also about love as ". . . a flash of certainty/ in the confused onslaught —" and the transformation of the body ". . . clean/ to the eye — ." The poem concludes with the aftermath of love, a stasis in which love is asserted against all the uncertainties in the world and in the relationship between men and women, always mysterious and enigmatic.

These poems are complemented by a group of later poems in which Williams touches on the theme of the virgin and the whore (although not until *Paterson* does he consciously use the image as he perceived it in his study of the French tapestries). His observation in "A Plea for Mercy," that all men *seek* an ideal of purity not possible in the real world leads to speculation:

> Who hasn't been frustrated
> with the eternal virgin
> shining before him and he
> cold as stone?

What men *find* is the virgin and the whore. In "To All Gentleness": "Out of
fear lest the flower be broken/ the rose puts out its thorns. . . ." Williams in-
dicts the world for its indifference, for its rapaciousness, for its loss of
"gentleness." He poses the conundrum: "Violence and/ gentleness, which is
the core?" and the final image of the poem is a personification of that paradox
in the form of the woman,

> She was
> forewoman to a gang at the ship foundry,
> . . . .
> Not the girth of thigh, but
> that gentleness that harbors all violence,
> the valid juxtaposition, one
> by the other, alternates, the cosine, the
> cylinder and the rose.

That gentleness is found in unexpected places is the poem's surprise: in "the
cylinder and the rose."

In "Eternity," Williams tells Elsie's story again: "She had come, like the
river/ from up country and had work now/ in town —" The young virgin-
turned-whore seems peculiarly vulnerable: ". . . She/ appeared/ bare-headed,
in pearl earrings/ and a cloak. Where shall/ we go?" The tryst is played out
against the darkness of the cosmos: ". . . And the stars performed/ their
stated miracles." Racing home in the night, the lover takes time to savor the
night, count the stars, note "the sky! velvet, like a leaf." As always the experience leaves him quiet, speculative, overwhelmed by the emotion of pity,
as the leaf suggests. For Williams often equated the fallen girl with the falling
leaf of autumn. He stops under a street lamp and scribbles some notes — the
poem?

Two other poems touch upon the image of the virginal whore: "3 A.M.
the Girl with Honey Colored Hair" and "The Clouds." In the first of these,
the girl with the honey-colored hair lights up the tawdry street, her hair il-
luminating the drunks, the hardened old whores, the human derelicts one
would find at 3 A.M. on a city street. The speaker concludes: "all/ were
affected as she/ turned frightened to address/ me pitifully alone." The image
of innocence, fear, loneliness, and shining beauty merge in the speaker's
imagination as he evokes the emotion of pity.

"The Clouds" is a somewhat longer poem, opening upon a city dawn
that resembles death more than life: "a rank confusion of the imagination
. . ." The images are dark and forbidding: "gigantic beasts/ rearing flame-
edged above the pit"; the ". . . smell of the swamp, a mud/ livid with decay

and life!...."; putridity and blindness. In this urban Hell, the poet dreams
of another age, the rich past of Villon and Erasmus and Shakespeare,
Aristophanes and Plato. Where are they now? They live still in ourselves,
he argues. He recalls Toulouse-Lautrec, who captured the beauty of whores,
and therein finds the answer for himself:

> ... Toulouse-Lautrec, the
>
> > deformed who lived in a brothel and painted
> > the beauty of whores. These were
> > the truth-tellers of whom we are the sole heirs

The speaker concludes:

> With each, dies a piece of the old life, which he carries,
> a precious burden beyond! Thus each
> is valued by what he carries and that is his soul—
> diminishing the bins by that much
> unless replenished.

The charge to the poet is clear: to join that brotherhood that replenishes life.
But the poem concludes with the beclouded vision of a sterile world hurtling
toward its death and disintegration, enclosing the poet within it. The poem
is a dark vision; as he will discover in his perambulations in the city of Paterson, that world is a tragic contemporary wasteland where love is absent,
language absent, communication lost, values dead. The only positive note
is felt in the presence of Toulouse-Lautrec, who raised that tarnished world
to art and saw goodness in seeming depravity. We are reminded that Book
V of *Paterson*, Williams' only affirmative vision, is dedicated "To the Memory
of Henri Toulouse-Lautrec, Painter."

Despite their infinite variety, Williams' women in these shorter poems
share certain qualities that will persist in the women of his later poems. If
the women are young, they are modern Venuses, luring the poet with their
beauty and sexuality. Their eyes are clear, often grey, and their heads and
arms and legs are bared to the elements. There is an aroma of healthy,
youthful seductiveness about them, and despite a bit of tawdriness from
cheap jewelry and glittering dresses, they betray a kind of innocence that in
no way diminishes their allure. If the women are old, they are worn-out
whores, kindly, clear-eyed, honest. They have a truth to teach and a
worldliness to impart. They guide the initiate and keep a gentleness for him.
In the light of day, they may be ugly and wasted, but a mysterious beauty
clings to them despite sunken breasts and wrinkled skin. The virgin contains
within her the potentiality of becoming the whore, and the whore retains
something clean and untouchable—something one may term "innocence."
The virgin and the whore, are, Williams would write in *Paterson*, an "identity." The speaker in "Venus Over the Desert" testifies to this truth as Venus
claims her presence in *all* women:

> If I do not sin, she said, you shall not
> walk in long gowns down stone corridors.
> There is no reprieve where there is no fall-
> ing off. I lie in your beds all night, from
> me you wake and go about your tasks.

Venus is both the virgin and the whore: an "identity." But it is this same
Venus whose love comforts all men in the face of their defeats and saves them
from the hypocrisy of empty virginity.

Since so much of Williams' early work reflects the biographical aspects
through which his two worlds converge, it is not surprising to find several
poems marking the events of death and life in his own family. Particularly,
the dying Elena haunted him, much as the dying grandmother would provide one of the most poignant poems in *Paterson*. Old though she was, blind
and crippled, Williams could recapture Elena as she was in youth. In two
poems, "Two Pendants for the Ears" and "Tribute to Neruda the Collector
of Seashells," there are sharp evocations of the emotions Elena roused
in him:

> You lean the head forward
> and wave the hand,
> with a smile,
> twinkling the fingers
> I say to myself
> Now it is spring
> Elena is dying

He touches again on the haunting tragedy of Elena's alienation: from the
tropics, from the mango and the guava, from the familiar and beloved.
Against the well-meaning denials of the family (for Elena, old, has been
dying for a long time), the poet intones,

> Elena is dying (I wonder)
> willows and pear trees
> whose encrusted branches
> blossom all a mass
> attend her on her way—

Elena is dying, and the doctor-son-poet feels winter in himself in April. The
irony of the birth of the year and the death of the mother is underscored
throughout the poem. Like the myth of Kore, springtime always carries with
it an aura of death, and the poet's imagination closes in on both. The poem
ends "Elena is dying," but the canary sitting on the breakfast table, nibbling
on the crumbs, is a fragile sign of new life. When we realize the degree to
which Williams identified his own state as alien, artist, iconoclast with Elena,
we sense the depth of his grief.

In the second poem, the poet — now old and blind and powerless like the powerless, dying Elena — retreats into himself. The poem begins on this personal note:

> Now that I am all but blind,
> however it came about,
> though I can see as well as anyone — the imagination
> has turned inward

As he had done over and over in the past, he tells her story: the childhood in Spanish-speaking Mayaguez. Her language was that of Neruda, who collected seashells on *his* native beach, as she might have as a child. So the mother (long dead), Neruda and the seashells, and the mind of the poet converge, artists all, concerned with changeless beauty like the sea itself. The poignancy of Williams' recollections of Elena came from his identification with the tragedy of her misspent life. That tragedy was his own fear, as he waited for the world to "receive" him and for the poetry to find its place.

In many ways, *Pictures from Brueghel* is both the volume of Williams' old age and "Flossie's Book." But many of the later short poems testify to the "flossiness" in Williams' life: order, sense, security, and protective love. Williams was often amusing, touching, gentle, and appreciative when he wrote about Flossie — and often realistic. As early as *Kora* he wrote:

> I have discovered that the thrill of first love passes! It even becomes the backbone of a sordid sort of religion if not assisted in passing. . . . I have been reasonably frank about my erotics with my wife. I have never or seldom said, my dear I love you, when I would rather say: My dear, I wish you were in Tierra del Fuego.[15]

But Flossie was the "normal" part of Williams' existence without which he would probably not have survived the chaos *and* the creativity. In two poems to Flossie, he makes his declaration of love to the world, the first in "Three Sonnets":

> In the one woman
> I find all the rest — or nothing

If "stealing" had its place, it had nothing to do with his abiding love for Florence Williams, and their long life together testifies to the success of their marriage — despite what dark moments we cannot know. Clearly, Flossie was ready to accept the "burial" of the innumerable women with courage and faith in Williams' assertion: "In the one woman/ I find all the rest."

In "The Flower" his love for Flossie calmly illuminates the lines as brightly as the sun where she sits:

> This too I love
> Flossie sitting in the sun

One is tempted to add, "God's in his heaven; all's right with the world," for the moment captured in the poem's few images — Flossie, a rose, a pet canary — conveys Williams' quintessential contentment. They were not frequent moments in his busy life as doctor, writer, poet, restless spirit; more so were they treasured moments. Though he had "discovered the thrill of first love passes," he was infinitely sensitive to what took its place: affection, comradeship, giving and taking, the joy of the "familiar" — in short, love.

It is fitting that I close this chapter on the women in Williams' early and later short poems with one that is a "Prologue" to *Paterson*. "Rogation Sunday" is a poem in the Kore motif and is an appeal, almost a prayer, for new life, a renewed spirit of brotherhood among men and women, a springtime returned. It is the closest Williams comes to a spiritual assertion, and it is grounded in the hope that all men may reap the harvest of "revival." The nurturing of the soil and the nurturing of the soul fuse in the poem, which celebrates the ritual of rebirth in Whitmanesque spirit. There are many moments of despair and pessimism in *Paterson*, but myth often culminates in a positive vision, and *Paterson* begins with that hope. Though Williams, especially in old age, frequently despaired of the world, his stubborn search for the "radiant gist" is augured in "Rogation Sunday." In this brief invocation, he reaches a rare moment of aspiration combined with a cheery conviction that we shall reap the harvest:

> O let the seeds be planted
> and the worry and unrest be invited!
> Let that which is to come
> of the weather and our own weakness
> be accepted!

In a way, the poem is a Maytime ritual. Williams brings together many of his earlier themes. The fruition of nature is produced by male and female, man and the fertile soil . . . that ritual that is the miracle of life. Repeatedly he calls for the seed to be planted as the central motif of the poem. Thus the harvest, not only rye and oat and corn, but joy and harmony and revival for man will result from this May planting. In the "Coda" to "Rogation Sunday," he poses a series of questions that synthesize all that man reaps from the harvest: the brotherhood of men, love and devotion, and the beauties of nature imaged in the woman who gave of herself. The poem celebrates revival and survival, for as the land returns, so does meaningful life for man.

Chapter V
Paterson: "Beautiful Thing"

"Rigor of beauty is the quest."

Paterson I

William Carlos Williams' long poem, *Paterson*, his American *Paradise Lost*, is a myth. Like Milton's great epic, it has to do with a paradisal past, the loss of Eden, and the search for its recovery: in sum, with life, death, and resurrection. Unlike Milton's religious work, there is no distinction between sacred and profane, no individualized culpability (the "first disobedience . . ." of which Milton wrote), no "fortunate Fall" enabling the coming of the Savior; but permeating the five books of *Paterson* and into the uncompleted sixth, there is a poignant nostalgia for an idyllic past when man and woman, nature and the creative imagination existed in perfect harmony. The need to recapture, if only in transient moments, the radiance of that union sends the poet on his quest: "But how will you find beauty when it is locked in the mind past all remonstrance?" Milton created his response in *Paradise Regained* and foreshadowed the coming of the Redeemer at the close of *Paradise Lost*. But Williams' "faith" is of another stamp — more evanescent and less conventional. It comes in "isolate flecks," unlocks the language of the mind and passions and opens up to the beauty beneath the surface of ordinary reality.

His poem rests on a myth that provides the scaffold for *Paterson*, its key images and motifs: the journey with Dr. Paterson from death to life. His transformation of the myth as an American vision is suited to the modern life he perceived around him.

I have noted elsewhere[1] that Williams lived astride two worlds: the prosaic world of Rutherford and the world of the imagination. The sometimes violent yoking of those polar worlds brings about their coexistence in what he called a *third* world, the poem, where each particular retains an integrity of its own, yet through invention can startle us anew. In this third world, Williams has created his myth of America.

Paterson has been called a "collage," a "mosaic," a "long poem in four parts,"[2] — none of which confronts the poem's complex structure, though all these descriptive terms are valid. If the poem contains an architectural frame, the clue can be found in the epigraph: "Rigor of beauty is the quest." All myths are essentially journeys in search of an abiding reality, a timeless, spaceless realm that is unified, indivisible, and self-contained. The presence of mythic elements in *Paterson* hints at such a structure: the archetypal journey, the omnipresence of the colossal giants, the wandering quester who must undergo an experience of isolation, initiation, and discovery as he searches the urban wasteland, history, myth, and legend for that impalpable "beauty locked in the mind past all remonstrance." And finally, the poem is structured on a recurrent theme of death and rebirth: descent and ascent, dispersal and metamorphosis.

But for Williams, myth was more than the stuff of mystics, metaphysicians, and mythopoeia. In the first place, the mythic absolute of sacred and profane was anathema to Williams, for whom there was no "other world" in any doctrinal sense. "Here is everywhere," he wrote, though the commonplace world of Rutherford is lit now and then by a radiant spark, while the perfect, immutable "sacred" quality is paradoxically fleeting—its harmony and wholeness yielding in an instant to a darker vision.

He asserted, "A life that is here and now is timeless. That is the universal I am seeking: to embody that in a work of art, a new world that is always 'real.' "[3] But even art had its limitations, as Guimond notes: "He did not believe that art could cure life's pain, ugliness, or deformities; but . . . Williams affirms that art can heal the effects these things have upon men's minds."[4]

So as we read *Paterson*, we experience the dark moments transformed by a flash of beauty, while the quest for beauty often brings us to the nadir of deformity, ugliness, and pain. The virgin and the whore are often indistinguishable; the sacred and profane often inextricable. *Paterson* rests, then, on a primordial myth of death and rebirth reflected in two classical archetypes: the Greek myth of Demeter/Kore and the myth of the temptation, capture, killing, and resurrection of the sacred unicorn, depicted in the French tapestries in the Cloisters.

The importance of woman in this American myth cannot be overstated. Mariani calls *Paterson V* "The Book of the Woman," but the entire work is haunted by women, both mythical and real: "Each like a flower."[5] In all her metamorphoses, woman is the object of the quest; it is with the woman that Paterson wishes union. If, on an allegorical level, he is the city, she is the land: rocky Garrett Mountain, the American soil. Marriage with her will effect the communion with beauty, the "radiant gist," the female principle of creativity and earthly and artistic fruition. But the woman is also the reality he seeks in the living world around him in all its tragedy and despair of betrayal. She is experience and love in all its variety, and she is that other part of *himself* for which he yearns as he wanders through the city streets, or the park, or the river's edge. Williams had written, characteristically, at the new year of 1911, in a letter to Viola Baxter, ". . . men are not strong enough to 'bat air' with women that forever proves to me I am not a man; they, men, disgust me and if I must say it fills me with awe and admiration. I am too much a woman."[6] We have only to recall Jung's observation of the naturalness of Williams' declaration: "The Kore figure is . . . an archetypal presence in both male and female."[7] She is the "immortal" part of himself that the wanderer in *Paterson* searches to recover. Paterson's "adventure" will therefore be one of novitiate, initiation, death, and rebirth—or in the terms

Williams will use — "descent" and "ascent"; in Book IV, he will actually undergo a "death" in the "sea of blood," from which he will miraculously "wade ashore."

Myth has a happy ending. Ernst Cassirer wrote:

> Over and over again we thus find confirmation of the fact that man can apprehend and know his own being only insofar as he can make it visible in the image of the gods. Just as he learns to understand the structure of his body and limbs only by becoming a creator of tools and products, so he draws from his spiritual creations — language, myth and art — the objective standards by which to measure himself and learn to understand himself as an independent cosmos with its peculiar structural laws.[8]

Williams might have made Eliot's rejoinder, "I do not know much about gods," but he coveted his "gods" as fiercely as though they were sacred idols: language, poetry, art. *Paterson's* hero is a mythic giant, awakened from the past like some Rip Van Winkle to recapture his lost world. The goddess upon whose bosom he has lain, still asleep in the confused modern world, will emerge as virgin and whore and will lead him back to her:

> So through art alone, male and female, a field of
> flowers, a tapestry, spring flowers unequaled
> in loveliness.

The beginning of *Paterson* not only places us in a particular time and a particular place — "a local pride; spring, summer, fall and the sea" — but creates the atmosphere of the cosmogonic act: "To make a beginning." Like Chaucer's spring, it is a season of promise and heralds the burgeoning life in nature and in man; thus it is fittingly a "celebration." But it will also be the "fall" and "the sea" — the one an intimation of the lost Eden, the other a faint evocation of both death and new life. The cyclical pattern will be composed of "a dispersal and a metamorphosis," a description not only of Paterson's perambulations in the city but a suggestion of organic change. The words intone the goal: "To make a start":

> For the beginning is assuredly
> the end —

The paradoxical tone is struck: searching for "pure and simple" we discover only our "complexities" — and the knowledge "fells us."

The poet's creation is revealed in Williams' most familiar analogy: the birth of a baby, the "nine months' wonder"; the preface emphasizes the difficulty of bringing his conception to fruition. To be born is first to die, repeating the cosmogonic act of chaos before life can emerge: ". . . rolling up out of chaos,"

> ... so that never in this
> world will a man live well in his body
> save dying —
>
> . . . .
>   ... Renews himself
> thereby ...

As the sea itself completes its own cycle of renewal in dispersal and metamorphosis, so will the man Paterson, the city, and the universe. The female principle, expressed in these opening lines, testifies to Williams' faith in the relationship between the process in nature and the process in art: Whittemore explains the relationship in this way: "Each of us creates the world even as it creates us and we must not seek to separate our private sensibilities from the big outside other."[9]

The transcendent aim of Williams' myth, a coherent world, appears at the outset, as the wanderer begins his quest for union with a source of creativity that will give value to his life, his city, his world, his art. The vehicle of communion will be the language, and the act of creation will be "invention," for without invention "it would all die voiceless."[10] Early in *Paterson*, he makes his commitment:

> Without invention nothing is well spaced,
> . . . .
>   ... unless there is
> a new mind there cannot be a new
> line, ...

In the first book of *Paterson*, the giant will awaken from his long sleep to the "thunder/ of the waters filling his dreams." The transformation from dream to the real world will be prefigured in the awakening of the seasonal cycle when the "cylindrical trees/ bent, forked by preconception and accident —/ split, furrowed, creased, mottled, stained — / secret — into the body of light!" It is a bleak awakening, reminiscent of the slowly surging life in "Spring and All." Yet the wanderer will awaken with his quest upon his lips:

> A man like a city and a woman like a flower
> — who are in love. Two women. Three women.
> Innumerable women, each like a flower.

It is Paterson's "innumerable women" who people his world and his imagination, and they are various and enigmatic as he pursues them and they pursue him. Benjamin Sankey has suggested only a few of their many associations, all of which appear in Book I and multiply throughout the remainder of his quest. They represent the "fallen world" — all that has been betrayed. They are mythic giants, flowers, and American wilderness ("mauled and raped by the invaders of Europe");[11] they are the Beautiful Thing. But they are more than Sankey suggests. They are the "pure products of America" gone crazy, the victims of urban deprivation and corruption. They are the young, giggling girls making love on Sunday in the park, and the old crones dancing vulgarly on the cliff. They are the overly curious Mrs. Cumming and the toughened Phyllis and the "creator," Madame Curie, and all of the virgins and whores Paterson encounters in his wanderings. They are depravity and beauty, but always they are redolent of eroticism, fecundity, the life force. And woven into the fabric of these often faceless, nameless women are the real women who constituted Williams: Emily Wellcome, Elena, Flossie, and ultimately the "female" in himself: "I give you . . . a young man/ sharing the female world."

The first part of Book I of *Paterson* takes place in the mythic American "garden." It is appropriate that in the season of procreation the first woman we encounter is the female giant resting against the sleeping hero. She is the embodiment of the earth, Demeter, but she conveys Kore's lush beauty. The embrace of the lovers—city and mountain—recalls the primordial paradise, the "reality" of the past—now only a dream. The giant goddess is the manifestation of the female principle without which the artist is incomplete. In his dreams, there is a quiet communion between them, but the awakening is painful, for it unfolds the whole degraded world. "Innumerable flowers" from "the back country" will meet degradation and shame in the city.

But almost immediately following this idyllic opening, we find a fragment of a letter from a woman we will come to know as "Cress," who berates Paterson for his supposed neglect. "Cress" is the literary alias for the young writer Marcia Nardi, whom Williams knew over a long period of years, appearing and disappearing in his life. Mariani credits Nardi with being the impetus for the writing of *Paterson*, that "wiry, diminutive, and bedraggled young woman who landed at Williams' office door" and whose letters castigating the poet for his indifference, his inhumanity to women, his treatment of her work are scattered through the poem. As Mariani noted, Nardi personified "the woman as victim, complaining, accusing, crying out in pain; the divorce between the sexes and the danger that the woman would turn to other women for solace; the woman as the energy and the flower old man's life. . . ."[12]

Garrett Mountain, the sleeping giant, is omnipresent, but the rape of the land is the tale *Paterson* unfolds; the idyllic past remains where it always was "in the beginning"—recoverable only in dreams or fleeting glimpses. Paterson leaps awake to witness the sterile planting, not unlike the opening of Eliot's *The Waste Land* where "April is the cruelest month." Recalling that women are flowers, we are soon aware of the failure in nature: the misspent insemination of the bee and the thwarting of birth. At first a beginning is awaited. The word "begin" for Williams, as we have seen, is sacred whether in the experience of nature or man. Here, as he images the initiation of the

spring in the interpenetration of the petals and the bees, the joy of that
creativity overcomes him. But it is soon aborted:

> They sink back into the loam
>   crying out
> — you may call it a cry
> that creeps over them, a shiver
>   as they wilt and disappear:
> . . . .
> The language is missing them
>   they die also
>   incommunicado.

The failure of the procreative process is followed by its parallel in human experience, in the violation of the innocent "Elsies"—the theme Williams
begins in *Spring and All* and reiterates throughout *Paterson*. The wanderer
observes the "girls from/ families that have decayed and/ taken to the hills:
no words."

Following the pain of this experience, the wanderer sinks back into
memory and evokes the primitive purity of the seminaked African chieftain
and his many wives. Though the young, almost virginal last wife is erect and
powerful with her "uppointed breasts," Paterson is more touched by the first
wife, with "careworn eyes/ serious, menacing—but unabashed; breasts/
sagging from hard use . . ." Here together are the virgin and the whore:
youth and age, innocence and experience—both "stab at the mystery of a
man." Williams was to write in the last part of *Paterson*:

> — every married man carries in his head
>   the beloved and sacred image
>   of a virgin
>   whom he has whored

The voyager moves backward in time and space, but he has yet to confront the reality of his world—an accusation made by the woman writer,
Cress, in one of her several letters to him. In the midst of these reveries, he
recalls the historical account of Sarah Cumming. Though married to a
minister and "blessed with a flattering prospect of no common share of Tem-
poral felicity," Sarah Cumming was doomed. Whether she walks, jumps, or
falls—and the mystery lies unsolved—Sarah's prospects come to a rapid end
as she hurtles over the falls to her death. We are told that she was "charmed,"
and the word is ominous. What mesmerized Sarah, one of the "innocents"
of *Paterson*, was the fulminating power of the falls—the surging life—that
proved too much for her. The falls destroy Sarah Cumming as violently as
Kore's rape at the hands of Hades. "Unministered," she plunges into the
waters and death. So too, more deliberately, did Sam Patch "leap," but his
body is found the following spring in an ice-cake; Sarah was recovered from

"the muddy swirl." Patch achieves a certain kind of resurrection, unlike the unfortunate Sarah. And Paterson? He too will ultimately leap into the river of life, urged, like Sarah, by the siren call of babbling falls. He too will have to plunge to his death, hoping to be recaptured by the earth waiting to receive him. But at this point in his quest, he is not yet ready for the experience.

Later, in his musings on the tragic Sarah, and directionless in an undirected world ("There is no direction. Whither? I/ cannot say . . ."), the wanderer momentarily awakens to an unexpected vision of delight in his prosaic Paterson: the young, virginal girls, twin Marys, hailing the coming of Easter, season of resurrection and renewal. As he had so often pictured the innocent girls in the earlier poems, they are unencumbered, ". . . bare-/ headed, their clear hair dangling — " They are "two" — a unity, coherence, an image of beauty:

> ribbons cut from a piece
> cerise pink, binding their hair: one —
> a willow twig pulled from a low
> leafless bush in full bud in her hand,
> (or eels or a moon!)
> holds it, the gathered spray,
> upright in the air, pouring air,
> strokes the soft fur —
>
> Ain't they beautiful!

Though he had found "Divorce is/ the sign of knowledge in our time,/ divorce! divorce!" the painful realization is suddenly relieved in this flash of pure beauty marked by union. True, innocence is short-lived in *Paterson*. "Virginity is a myth — ask any child of three."[13] Mrs. Cumming shrieked and fell, but the young, half-grown girls and the African's first wife stab at the heart of a man. He yearns for his own "first wife," affirming her flowerlike beauty and perfection in broken language as he evokes her from dreams, "a flower within a flower." He has awakened to death and thwarted life in *Paterson*, but the flower within a flower holds the promise of that first experience. Paterson continues on his quest, secure in his memory of "a first beauty."

Returning to the thoughts of his first wife, Paterson envisages the love scene of the perfect lovers, the elemental giants. The scene is a remarkable contrast to the mundane world of the city. The lovers are able to sit and talk; he confirms their sexual communion, their marriage, their quiet moments when speech is superfluous "beneath the quiet heaven of/ your eyes." To seize the moment is a kind of death as the lover will "fall —/ with you from the brink, before/ the crash — ." The experience seems an image of the leap into death of Mrs. Cumming and Sam Patch, but it is a "death" that promises rebirth. They speak of resurrection:

> We sit and talk and the
> silence speaks of the giants
> who have died in the past and have
> returned to those scenes unsatisfied
> and who is not unsatisfied . . .

The silence of the sleeping giants is ominous; paradoxically they do not awaken and share the hopes of Patch and Mrs. Cumming.

As this second part concludes, there is little *proof* of resurrection, only the overwhelming presence of death. What lies before Paterson's eyes is the perversion of Elena's homeland, the fears of a woman who is convinced her husband means to kill her, the delirium, depravity, and degradation of the whorehouse forcing Paterson into back streets, up hollow stairs, to the obscene rendezvous. Finally, this part of the poem ends with an accusation by a fellow writer that Williams is separating art and life. True, his concept — to unite his worlds — has resulted in "divisions and imbalances," and the passage ends in defeat.

In Part Three, Paterson is still in the season of early spring, hopefully awaiting the blossoming of the rose. While the rose calls up traditional suggestions, it is here Williams' favorite equation: "a woman in a flower." That the green rose will bloom is the promise of sexual fulfillment held out to him.

> And his thoughts soared
> to the magnificence of imagined delights

The green/red rose conveys paradoxical evocations: green is the color of youth, perhaps virginity, the potentiality for fruition. Red is the perfected maturity, experience. Again, the duality of the rose suggests the virgin and the whore, one exciting his anticipation of purity and potential, the other suggestive of erotic sensations: "his mind drinks of desire." The world itself is a rose that will open and close to him — a sexual metaphor — and will never wither permanently, as he declares in Book II. Instead, it will move through the cycle of life, death, and rebirth as the flower itself moves through its seasonal cycle:

> . . . The world spreads
> for me like a flower opening — and
> will close for me as might a rose —
>
> wither and fall to the ground
> and rot and be drawn up
> into a flower again. But you
> never wither — but blossom
> all about me. . . .

Both passages are testaments of faith in the constant cycle of birth and death and resurrection, so that as Paterson declares, "We go on living, we permit ourselves/ to continue— ..." The you who will never wither is the female lover, the eternal earth.

The wanderer continues, sensitive to the desire for rebirth all around him: in the woman who asks him to give her a baby, in Sam Patch who leaps forward toward his fate: death and resurrection, a "sort of springtime":

> "... the body, not until
> the following spring, frozen in
> an ice cake"

Paterson envies Patch, but is still unable to leap into his world and find new life. His walk has been a kind of sleep-walking in which he records his contemporary world but is unable to mitigate its suffering.

Book I of *Paterson* ends in failure since the quester, repelled by what he sees in his real world, fearful, and impotent to change it, sinks into a mood of indifference. Paterson's instinct is one of flight, away from the ugliness of the sewer that is modern civilization. He drives away in his car, turning his back upon the vulgar streets, the blank and staring eyes, the senseless rapes, but noting for a fleeting moment:

> Plaster saints, glass jewels
> and those apt paper flowers, bafflingly
> complex—have here
> their forthright beauty, beside:

Once again, the instant of surprise—the presence of beauty amid the squalor of the modern streets with their "paper flowers": the virginal whores.

In Book II, Paterson doggedly sets out again on his quest. Returning to his beloved Garrett Mountain, he finds it despoiled and vulgarized, but he is determined to search "outside/ outside myself/ there is a world." Paterson finds himself in a park on a Sunday afternoon in late spring. The season and the place hold out new hope for the inhabitants of the city on this day of "rebirth," but the experience "fells" him as he wanders among the contemporary scenes of lovemaking and violence. He discovers that love is debased: the spring is "too late" though the creatures in nature go about their rites of rebirth: the birds nesting, "churring" their celebration of new life: "couriers to the ceremonial of love!" The picnickers in the park dance and sing and copulate, but there seems to be no communication, and the description of their intercourse is repellent, vulgar, unrelieved by love. Black or white, the whores have usurped the park, and the goddess sleeps beneath the grass.

Yet another surprise awaits Paterson, for as he strolls among the lovers, he notes they are "Not undignified ... talking flagrant beyond all talk/ in perfect domesticity—/ And having bathed/ and having eaten (a few/ sand-

wiches)/ their pitiful thoughts do meet/ in the flesh — surrounded/ by churring loves!. . ." That a spark of something "dignified" can be found in this
"frank vulgarity" is part of Paterson's education in his real world.

For a fleeting moment he finds peace and pleasure in the dancing feet
of the Sunday joy-seekers. They clamber over the sleeping goddess, and for
one magical instant, "the imagination soars, as a voice/ beckons, a thundrous
voice, endless/ as sleep:. . ." The people, unknowingly, and Paterson re-
spond to the summons. In answer, "the mountain quivers." The dance of the
old crone, Mary, that follows is a celebration, a rite of spring. Though the
old whore *seems* vulgar and though her motions are flagrantly erotic, the
dance between the female and the male (the satyr) is a fertility rite:

> —the leg raised, verisimilitude
> even to the coarse contours of the leg, the
> bovine touch! The leer, the cave of it,
> the female of it facing the male, the satyr —
>   (Priapus!)
> with that lonely implication, goatherd
> and goat, fertility, the attack, drunk,
> cleansed

Paul Mariani, in his discussion of Mary, the dancing crone, has sen-
sitively analyzed her dance in light of other reverberations, mythic and
biographic, that always lie beneath the surface of Williams' "crones." Mary's
dance, he writes:

> . . . is a movement, a whirring of wings, an annunciation as
> Mary — in her traditional black dress — brings to this scene a language
> of her own, a local dialect. . . . And now, as Mary begins to dance, the
> language too catches fire, the dance of the language moving with its
> own grace in time to the gaiety of the woman's steps. . . . 'Look a' me,
> Grandma!' Williams has Mary say, though it is a private joke as well,
> Williams invoking his own first muse, Grandmother Wellcome, who
> had taught him the language. And the gesture, identical with the dance
> everywhere as in the image of the goddess older than the other — Shiva,
> her head too cocked, hand held high with cymbals . . . dancing, though
> she did not know it, with the poet who has discovered her here and
> dances her into the heart of his poem.[14]

The dance of renewed life is imitated in the sordid copulation of the lovers
in the park. Repelled again, Paterson falls asleep; he dreams of a union with
the female spirit of the mountain, and, as frequently in Williams' poetry, the
act of love becomes an act of rebirth.

>   reborn
> in his sleep — scattered over the mountain
> severally
>
>   — by which he woos her, severally.

Once more, Paterson escapes, his quest unfulfilled in the real world as he sinks into the oblivion of sleep with its dream of rebirth and dispersal.

The second part of Book II documents Paterson's paralysis. Unable to take any meaningful action, still "undirected," he can only walk in the city clinging to the faith that the answer lies with woman, ". . . sick of his diversions, but proud of women." But his failure with women is borne out in the accusing letter from Cress, whom he has rejected. The attack on contemporary values diverts him further from his quest, as he rails against America's materialism, the betrayal of its people, its false worship of religion. Paterson sinks to despair, though it is here he affirms the cycle of the rose and his conviction that "you" — Garrett Mountain — "never wither." The passage ends with an even stronger indictment from Cress.

It is the last part of Book II that holds the key to Paterson's "direction." The hints have been present all along in the image of Sam Patch's death and "resurrection," in the cycle of the rose and of the sea, in the patterns of dispersal and metamorphosis. Here for the first time in *Paterson* the cyclical design in nature is superimposed upon the cycle of man's life, even as the falls must "chatter" man's doom. Spring arrives with its flowers, to be followed by the litany of death and rebirth. What saves man? For Williams, always the same sources of rebirth: memory, desire, and love.

> The descent beckons
>   as the ascent beckoned
>   Memory is a kind
> of accomplishment
>   a sort of renewal
>   even
> an initiation, since the spaces it opens are new
> places
> . . . .
> The descent
>   made up of despairs
>   and without accomplishment
>
> realizes a new awakening   :
>   which is a reversal
> of despair.

The pattern of Kore's death and rebirth, and Williams' own identification with the Greek maiden, reinforces his belief in the design of ascent and descent that governs the poem and the spiritual state of the quester, who alternately despairs and accomplishes. Through memory (in his dream life with the female giant, in his recreation of the city's beginnings and its history, in his nostalgia for the past) he has touched a "sort of renewal" though the rebirth in the real world yet awaits him. Spring will come, and this is the reassurance to carry the voyager-poet through his descent and ascent. Both movments are necessary for life and art, neither to be averted or denied.

But the character, Paterson, has not fully comprehended what the poet knows to be true. Paterson has yet to leap into the filthy Passaic, to face his own world and his own nothingness. Until this point, he has been the "observer," participating only in dreams. There is still much to see in his novitiate, as the crone in "The Wanderer" has warned him before he yields to the virgin and the whore.

At the close of Book II, his inner voice warns him: "Be reconciled, poet, with your world, it is/ the only truth." Complaining that "—the language is worn out," he is answered by the female giant: "You have abandoned me!" Summer has come, and the time is slipping away. He has a vision of his lover, a seductive Venus tempting him:

Her belly	.	her belly is like
a cloud	.	a cloud
		At evening .

but on this ". . . most voluptuous night of the year," the ". . . blood is still and indifferent, . . ." His failure to live and love are most bitterly decried in a long letter from the abandoned woman Cress. "You never had to live, Dr. P. — not in any of the by-ways and dark underground passages where life so often has to be tested. . . . I wanted your friendship more than I ever wanted anything else." The dark, underground passages still await him, as he suffers the destructive consequences of his indifference to the ordinary life around him.

Book III opens in the heat of summer at its height, and Paterson escapes into the cool library to lose himself in solitude from the oppressive city and its tragic squalor. The books will cool the senses. Here, at the center of the poem, Paterson is hypnotized by the object of his quest: Beautiful Thing. Mariani finds the source for Beautiful Thing in Williams' memories of Mabel Watts, "the seductive patient from his early days as doctor," a woman who had as much sexual "success with white men as with black."[15] At first, she evokes locust blossoms with their mesmerizing perfume. She is a woman, a flower, an emblem of life, offering a merciful stasis to Paterson, who is "spent from wandering the useless/ streets these months . . ." She is his dove, wind-blown, "—a dark flame,/ a wind, a flood—counter to all staleness," who will scourge the modern world of its desolation and stagnation—even here in the library of dead men's dreams.

The motif of the purging fire is traceable to the myth of the Phoenix and in all the literature of religion, from the great fires of St. Augustine and Buddha to Dante's *Purgatorio* and, more recently, to Eliot's "Little Gidding" in *Four Quartets*. That the fire of beauty will ultimately destroy the library and the "doomed city" will be developed in the passage that follows, but here in the earlier passage of Book III, the Beautiful Thing becomes metamorphosed into the whored virgin, sacrificial victim of modern city violence. For the first time, Paterson not only sees beauty, but feels love and compassion in the real world, and it fells him. He sees her first in her "white dress"—emblem of inviolability:

> Haunted by your beauty (I said),
> exalted and not easily to be attained, the
> whole scene is haunted:

What follows is the love scene, complicated by his ambivalence. He is "haunted" by the quietness of her face, struck by her beauty, unattainable, and then turns in fury on her:

> Take off your clothes and purify
> yourself   .   .
> And let me purify myself
> . . . .
>   —that you might
> send me hurtling to the moon
>   .   .   let me look at you (I
> said, weeping)

Beautiful Thing is both the virgin and the whore, indivisible, calling up emotions of passion, pity, repugnance, astonishment. In one line Williams brings his theme of the oxymoron before us: ". . . the astonishing virtue of your/ lost body," and he reflects:

> What is there to say? save that
> beauty is unheeded   . tho' for sale and
> bought glibly enough

But Beautiful Thing's "gift" is beyond measure: "For what is there but love, that stares death/ in the eye, begetting marriage—" What Paterson learns from Beautiful Thing is that the ". . . Saintlike" can never be separate from ". . . that stain of sense": "Never that radiance/ quartered apart." And so the ". . . poet (ridded) from Paradise" finds ". . . that radiant gist" in the pitchblende, the virgin of his ideal in the whore, the Beautiful Thing. The remainder of this passage in Book III raises to dignity the dross of the city, the whore, as Toulouse-Lautrec before him had immortalized her in his art. The quester welcomes the dissolution of his world and himself to be reborn. "Death lies in wait,/ a kindly brother—/ full of the missing words."

What follows is the fire that sweeps over all. Beautiful Thing is the personification of that cleansing power, as I have noted, and swallows up everything in her wake: "Beautiful Thing! aflame   ." That the flame of beauty and the flame of love were synonymous was an early equation in

Williams' mind. He had written to Viola Baxter in 1911: "... the Repellent Flame is merely love, always powerful, always active, never to be denied. Men know it as babies know the Mother — as a place.... It is a force which can be felt, it is multiform — I have felt it command me in opposite ways ... that its purpose be accomplished."[16]

All the artifacts of culture are caught up in the conflagration, but the poet exults at her beauty, a vulgar beauty more precious than perfection. Once again, the virgin/whore exacts a kind of divine retribution; her powers, we were told, are the wind, the flood, the flame — nature's own tools of absolute destruction:

> Vulgarity surpasses all perfections
> — it leaps from a varnish pot and we see
> it pass — in flames!

Like Arnaut Daniel and the pilgrim, in *Purgatorio*, beauty itself experiences the purgatorial process, and Paterson sees the Beautiful Thing "scarred, fire swept":

> Rising, with a whirling motion, the person
> passed into the flame, becomes the flame —
> the flame taking over the person

She is "Beautiful Thing/ the flame's lover —" Thus concludes Paterson's vision of destruction by fire.

Beautiful Thing has been transformed into the purifying fire, but when next we see her, she has metamorphosed again into the vision of ruined innocence victimized by the city gang of toughs. Paterson visits her, as the doctor, and the thought of the raped Persephone comes to his mind. "Persephone/ gone to hell, that hell could not keep with/ the advancing season of pity." It is the Kore myth that stirs his imagination and the promise of resurrection for the degraded, mauled body lying on the bed. But, as I have noted earlier, he is still "Shaken by her beauty" as she lies in the squalor "... among the scabrous/ dirt of the holy sheets," the whored virgin. Beaten as a child, "maled" and "femaled" by the guys from Paterson or the guys from Newark, the "dove" of beauty is betrayed by the world. The realization is a bitter one for Paterson. As he gazes upon her, he is overcome with his own feelings of gentleness, tenderness, speechlessness; he wishes to brighten the corner where the "black plush," the Beautiful Thing, languishes.

> But you!
> — in your white lace dress
>   "the dying swan"
> ....
>   — a flame,
> black plush, a dark flame.

It is significant that before this final portrayal of the degradation of Beautiful Thing, the poet recalls the myth of the unicorn, also victimized — conversely by the virgin who tempted and betrayed him. Thus the tragedy of the captured holy unicorn is prefigured here in the tragedy of Beautiful Thing. The promise of resurrection that completes the tapestry series is missing here as Paterson, inarticulate and impotent, can envision only death and dishonor.

The final passage in Book III is a bleak recognition that "We walk into a dream, from certainty to unascertained . . ." so that Paterson is tempted once more to opt out of a world too painful to confront:

> But somehow a man must lift himself
> again —

So Paterson seeks a new beginning: "How to begin to find a shape — to begin to begin again." But he can only dwell on the past; and, as the book concludes with the language of the falls cascading ". . . into the/ invisible, beyond and above: . . ." Paterson pledges to find his meaning, to "comb out the language — or succumb." The season of winter, death, lies before him and it is those emblems of the dead season that pass before his eyes as, still wandering, he seeks the language and communion and rebirth.

But if winter is the season of death in the land, it is also the season of birth in Christian myth, promising the resurrection. Too often, this is glossed over in the scholarly exegeses of Book IV of *Paterson*. True, the poem begins with images of disorder, confusion, perversion, and Paterson's own yearning for death in the "sea of blood." But there are flashes of the life surge, of "invention," of the creative element in both man and nature. Most significantly, Paterson is *not* dead at the close of Book IV, although he has experienced a symbolic death in the sea:

> mother in whom the dead, enwombed again
> cry out to us to return!

Book IV of Paterson begins with an "idyl" — Williams' satiric comment on a form of poetry so divorced from life that it contains no relevance to reality. This "idyl" takes place, as Guimond describes it succinctly, in a lost and dead world:

> The Passaic River is totally polluted and loses itself in Newark
> Bay. Human life, both male and female, is lost in the "perverse confu-
> sions" engendered by the abuses of power described in the previous
> Books. . . . The "words" of the poem . . . are perverted like the river.[17]

Against such a scene, we are introduced to the lesbian, Corydon, and the virgin, Phyllis, the nurse who both encourages and repels the seduction by the rich old lesbian and Paterson's equally inept advances. The passage probably goes on too long to make its point, but clearly the repulsive game of tempt and rebuff amuses the tough little nurse and disillusions the quester, who sees the "virgin" as some kind of modern tease who plays the sexual game with no promise of consummation. Simply because Phyllis preserves her virginity is no reason to admire her, Paterson discovers, and none of his descriptions of her ever approach the pity or empathy he felt as he beheld the broken body of Beautiful Thing. Phyllis' contempt for Paterson is clear, as is the inanity of her conversation: "You think I'm a virgin./ Suppose I told you/ I'd had intercourse. What/ would you say then?" Love, Paterson discovers, is ". . . begrimed, befouled." It is a sign of impotence and death. The section ends with both Corydon and Paterson wondering about Phyllis' "virginity." The knowledge seems pointless, for in her heart Phyllis is a temptress, a whore. She repels him. As Williams noted, Book IV

> shows the perverse conclusions that come of failure to untangle the language and make it our own as both man and woman are carried helplessly toward the sea (of blood) which, by their failure of speech awaits them. The poet alone in this world holds the key to their final rescue.[18]

Part two offers a hint of that final rescue as prefigured in the account of Madame Curie. In her lonely Paris garret, amidst the squalor of her city, Madame Curie dreams of her own creation. The account of her discovery of radium is imaged in the birth of a life: "a woman waiting to be filled/ — a luminosity of elements, the/ current leaping!" As the embodiment of the female principle, she is "pregnant," waiting to bring forth the uranium from the pitchblende. Williams continues with the image of pregnancy: her belly grows ". . . full/ of thought!. . .")"; after months of "labor," the birth — at night — (when most of Williams' babies were born!) the emergence of the luminous. Madame Curie's creation testifies to order, perfection, new life: "Curie woman (of no importance) genius: radium/THE GIST." In work, he concludes ". . . value created and received,/ 'the radiant gist' against all that/ scants our lives." So Paterson finds in his real world a bastion against "all that scants our lives." The passage ends on a note of triumph; as long as his contemporary world contains the life surge that led to Madame Curie's great invention, there is still reason to continue the quest. This returns him to his own invention: language. A voice asks, "Haven't you forgot your virgin purpose,/ the language?" Paterson still searches for the ideal, the pure, the living language that will make possible communion with his world. But he is still asleep, living in the past his grandmother warned him to relinquish: "The past is for those who lived in the past . . . ," not the living! The yawning ocean calls him to death as he questions the ability of giving birth in old age: "— and did you ever know of a sixty year/ woman with child   .?" He is that sterile old woman. As the tide beckons him, he reflects on the virtue of his quest: is it enough to wait for that "virtue" to come slowly, or is it enough simply to aspire; is virtue sufficient in the effort? Paterson is lethargic, though for a fleeting moment he has a vision of Venus rising on her shell, an image of renewal and desire. He recalls his grandmother, Emily Wellcome, still the tutelary spirit, and her words: "Virtue, she would say ./ is a stout old bird,/ unpredictable ..." Emily's virtue was something to be sought, caught, even when "unpredictable." But weakness overcomes Paterson, and he falls into reverie, recalling all the women he has known with their different names, "each like a flower": Margaret and Lucille, and Alma, and Nancy, but they were all victims in the world of Paterson, virgins-turned-whores, entrapped by the degraded city, fallen "Elsies" from the "back country":

> ... All these
> and more — shining, struggling flies
> caught in the meshes of Her hair ...

None can escape the rapacious in the wasteland city; all of the fallen are too vulnerable, too innocent, "half-awakened" to the evil around them ... lost.

Falling back further into the past, into death and further from present life, Paterson recreates the birth of his city in all its primitive purity and beauty: "Dominated by the Falls the surrounding country/ was a beautiful wilderness where mountain pink/ and wood violet throve ..." But today, "the sun goes beyond Garrett Mountain/ as evening descends ..." and "... It is as dark/ as Egypt." His dream of the past continues to draw him back into a kind of death, but even there he discovers death, rape, violence. He struggles to awaken, but the nirvana impulse seems to draw him into the sea of blood; the same sea bears "seeds," and in the image of words, new words, he seeks the seeds of renewal. The quester rejects death in the sea and evokes instead the sea's chief emblem of life: Venus, rising on the shell, rose pink. The experience is crucial, for having gone through an initiation of dispersal, of the death of the mind, the body, the poem itself, Paterson affirms rebirth — as always in his poetry, in the image of a woman, a temptress, Venus, the virgin and the whore:

> You will come to it, the blood dark sea
> of praise. You will come to it, Seed
> of Venus, you will return   . to
> a girl standing upon a tilted shell, rose
> pink   .

And so Paterson wades ashore. He's no sea-dog. The emergence on the shore, characteristically, is greeted by the frisking bitch dog and by his awareness of the "girls, far down on the beach, playing ball." The close of Book IV is enigmatic and seems to suggest death, until we think of the action

of the somersault; but the images of the spiral and the somersault both suggest circularity, return, and rebirth. The final words, "the end," might be the
end of Paterson's initiation of descent; but they might also be the "objective" — the end toward which he has been journeying in his quest for the
"beauty locked in the mind past all remonstrance." They might also be the
end of *Paterson*, for Williams had announced his work as four books. There
is a reflection of this ambiguity in the critical literature, since Williams
himself had announced the death of his hero at the beginning. Thirlwall
touches on this ambiguity:

> The hero is dead (the river has entered the sea, where it loses its
> identity); his death is attributable to a failure of language. Or is he
> dead? He "swims in" and strikes inland.... And in striking inland he
> is "answering" the challenge of the Falls, as reiterated by the sea.[19]

I would suggest that the design of "descent and ascent" in Book III is a prophecy of Book IV; Paterson is not dead, as the frisking dog testifies, and he
hears the voices of the nymphs on the beach — calling to him, calling him
back to life. He is himself a kind of Venus, emerging from the sea, returning
to his quest, his "end." He merges with the life force as he anticipates another
spring.

> The poet is now an old man, sure that his has been the right way,
> that through love for his world (it is both "virgin and whore") a poet may
> save it from the past for which it yearns and the future which it fears.[20]

Book V of *Paterson*, despite Williams' earlier plan for four books,
demanded to be written. It is again the season of procreation, but Paterson's
own northern spring, March, when the land is struggling to be renewed.
Like human birth, it is slow, painful, fragile, but a birth nonetheless. Paterson is in old age, himself struggling to recapture the flowers of his springtime
through remembering. He listens to the sounds of new life around him: the
song of the fox sparrow, the running of the streams, the language of the bare
rocks. It is the voice of his lover, Garrett Mountain, summoning him back
to the burgeoning season, the "thing itself!" not prophecy. As Guimond has
noted, the themes of Books I to IV — man's need for the new and woman's
need for constancy — had culminated in divorce. Book V, Guimond goes on
to demonstrate, is the renewal of love: ". . . if a man use his imagination to
keep his love vital, despite the material loss of her virginity, novelty, beauty,
and youth, he must be able to identify imaginatively with the virgin and the
whore."[21] Thus the theme of the virgin/whore dominates Book V, and Paterson will encounter her in all her manifestations.

Paterson V testifies to the impact that the fable of the unicorn and the lady
had on Williams' imagination. He found in this tale a betrayal of innocence
that was comparable to the abduction and violation of Persephone. The story

had recurred in ancient and medieval literature and art since 400 B.C. Margaret B. Freeman[22] traces the fable through its complex and fascinating history in the art and literature of ancient Greek, Roman, Judaic, and Christian cultures. From its beginnings, the fable accrued in meaning, picking up various and conflicting symbolism. Most often pictured in art, the unicorn also appears in literary accounts in the Greek *Physiologus*, in the Latin *Physiologus*, and in both the New and Old Testaments.

The most succinct version of the fable of the unicorn and the virgin was found in 1845 by Ludwig Uhland. Believed to be a medieval song, it recounts the events of the tale. The translation by Odell Shepherd is appended,[23] but significantly, the lines of the betrayal are central:

> And only a virgin's magic power
> Shall tame his haughty heart.

The story is a simple one in its main outlines. The unicorn, a one-horned, beautiful white beast in the shape of a horse, wanders in the idyllic hills until sought by hunters who witness the animal's magic powers; he dips his horn into a poisoned stream, purifying the water for the rest of nature's kingdom. The hunters pursue him with dogs and spears, but he succeeds in eluding them. They resort to a ruse by tempting him with a maiden. He permits her to fondle him and rest her hand on his mane. Hypnotized by love, he allows himself to be enclosed by a rose-covered fence and is subsequently killed. In some versions, the maiden witnesses the killing; in others she is absent. In several paintings, he is resurrected to live in an enclosure, tied to a tree bearing pomegranates.

The qualities that characterize the unicorn adhere to familiar Christian and secular symbolism, and like many medieval legends do not seem disturbing in their antithesis. The unicorn's beauty and innocence, his miraculous powers, his fierceness in resisting capture, his humility, his invincibility, and his final capitulation to be "tamed" by love are predominant traits of Christ.

Thus, in the Christian reading of the fable, the unicorn comes to symbolize Christ: he is sacrified and resurrected. In the Latin *Physiologus*, written in the ninth century, the unicorn springs into the lap of the maiden and embraces her; thus "In this way our Lord Jesus Christ, the spiritual unicorn, descended into the womb of the virgin and took on human flesh." The maiden is always taken for Mary, although, as Freeman notes, no one seemed disturbed that she would trick her only son to his death.

But the secular version of the fable was by far the more popular, especially in the Middle Ages. In one version (Pseudo-Hugo of St. Victor), an early erotic note is introduced in the unveiling of the beautiful maiden's breast. In other accounts, such as that by the abbess Hildegard von Bingen, several maidens entice the unicorn, who falls prey to their beauty and delight. But perhaps the best-loved version of the unicorn and his lady is told in the fourteenth century *Physiologus* and the medieval bestiaries. Here, it is primarily a love story celebrating temptation, love, death, rebirth, and marriage.

But it was the fifteenth-century tapestries in the halls of the Cloisters that William Carlos Williams knew so well. Clearly, the French tapestries combine both Christian and secular associations. The series is made up of seven facets of the fable: I. The start of the hunt; II. The unicorn dips his horn into the stream to rid it of poison; III. The unicorn leaps the stream; IV. The unicorn defends himself; V. The unicorn is tamed by the maiden; VI. The unicorn is killed and brought to the castle; VII. The unicorn in captivity. This last tapestry is accorded to be the masterpiece of the series, with the white Unicorn, miraculously resurrected, framed by the *millefleurs*. The scene evokes the colors of spring and renewal of life.

However, it is the fifth tapestry that most interested Williams, and, tragically, this tapestry is preserved only in fragmentary form. The full figure of the maiden who tames the unicorn is absent: "All that is visible of the maiden is a bit of her brocaded sleeve and her hand delicately caressing the Unicorn's mane. Her pert lady companion beckons, apparently to the hunter blowing his horn, to signal that the Unicorn may now be taken."[24] The interesting aspect here is the presence of not one but *two* maidens, and the one in full view is described by Freeman as intriguingly seductive with a sly expression. Here, symbolically, is the virgin and the whore, and so Williams interpreted the tapestry to demonstrate. Other details suggest the duality of the scene. The flowers are roses, lilies, and violets — frequently associated with the Virgin Mary; however, there is much erotic symbolism as well. The rose itself is a symbol of sensuous pleasure; the apple tree in the tapestry calls up all the connotations of the forbidden fruit and the fall from innocence. Freeman notes:

> Since the Unicorn in the lap of the maiden was the symbol of the lover captivated by his beloved, the apple tree in the Cloister's tapestry may be intended to suggest the sweetness of worldly love, as well as to recall the sin of Adam and Eve and Christ's incarnation.[25]

For Williams the tapestries would incarnate the cycle of his often-observed experience in nature and in man: life/death and violation, and rebirth. The fable evoked the already familiar myth of Kore. (Remarkable similarities exist between the two ostensibly different stories.) The image of the virgin/whore as it was filtered through Williams' imagination became a far more complex and enigmatic symbol, totally devoid of moral judgment and closer in spirit to the polar figures of Greek and Roman myth.

Paul Mariani in his essay "The Virgin and the Whore"[26] explores the fable of the virgin's pursuit and betrayal of the unicorn and Williams' use of the material he found in the Cloisters' tapestries. Like the unicorn, Mariani believes, Williams felt he'd been "hunted down by the dogs of his own thoughts even as he pursued the dream of the woman, the impossibly beautiful poem. The woman had lured him now for fifty years with her promises, and now she would finally call for his death." But the tale, it must be recalled, held the promise of rebirth. However, as Mariani notes, "Williams' retelling of the myth takes the form of the artist's imagination in pursuit of the woman, unabashed, naked pursuit after the poem, after the virgin language which must of necessity be whored, mauled, possessed by the lover, the poet." Williams had written Edward Dahlberg, who reminded him of the theme of the virgin/whore, that the final reconciliation of the various aspects of woman could be found in the figure of the "Virgin Mary, that whore, that glorious whore adored by the ages into perpetuity." Mary was to be honored not for her "perpetual chastity . . . but because she had given herself to her lover." As Mariani notes, "The virgin and the whore: the woman as artist, generator of myths, as well as mythic generator," confirms the identity of all women as one Woman.

In a letter to James Laughlin on the composition of *Paterson III* Williams wrote:

> Paterson is a man (since I am a man) who dives from cliffs and the edges of waterfalls, to his death — finally. But for all this he is a woman (since I am not a woman) who *is* the cliff and the waterfall. She spreads protecting fingers about his as he plummets to his conclusion to keep the winds from blowing him out of his path. But he escapes, in the end, as I have said.[27]

The relation between the creative imagination "to scatter his element recklessly" and the woman who harbors the "creative force and nurtures it" has been noted by James Guimond[28] and Hillis Miller[29] as a source of conflict in Williams' poetry. I would argue that the sexual response was a strong thread in Williams' poetry from the beginning, but that man's need for freedom and woman's need for constancy were the basis for a mutual relationship predicated on the existence of dual impulses in the poet himself. It is through his imagination that these twin impulses complement and renew each other. If the virgin is the desired woman, as Guimond suggests, and the male unicorn is destined to seek her, abuse her, and despoil her, then the "whore" becomes equated with "living fully." Guimond emphasizes this by suggesting that in *Paterson V* "a virgin is often downrightfully a whore in her own mind." Even "the most honorable husband 'whores' his wife; and so instead of being guilty, he should continue to love and cherish her in his imagination."

The theme of the virgin and the whore is translated, as Hillis Miller believes, into the possession of the world by possessing a beautiful woman —

"and the stain of love permeates the world." Miller concludes, "Williams' works taken all together make a poem which is a woman."[30]

Thus the myth of the betrayal of the unicorn figures largely in the fifth book of *Paterson*. The chief characters are the aged unicorn (Paterson himself) and the virgin/whore who will effect his capture, destruction, and resurrection. Her appearance is prefigured in Lorca's play in which the young girl leads her bridegroom to his downfall. We are told that the girl "innocently enough" was ". . . a hot little bitch . . ." — the virgin and the whore of Lorca's play leading to Paterson's reflections on purity and experience. As I noted earlier, Book V is dedicated to Toulouse-Lautrec, who immortalized the *poules* of Paris. So we find ourselves with Paterson in the whorehouse, where he argues the "moral" of the virgin and the whore:

> The moral
> proclaimed by the whorehouse
> could not be better proclaimed
> by the virgin, a price upon her head,
> her maidenhead!

The potentiality of the young bride to become the whore, the indivisibility of innocence and experience, the impossibility of retaining the ideal of a Beatrice or a Juliet in the real world is the moral proclaimed by the whorehouse. The world is a whorehouse, for only in the world of experience does Paterson live out his quest. He will find in the prosaic city the stuff of art, language, as the weavers of the tapestries had transformed experience into art, as had Stein and Klee, Dürer and Bosch, Freud, Picasso, and Juan Gris.

Much of the early part of the poem recounts the events of the unicorn's betrayal by the virgin:

> The Unicorn
> . . . .
> faceless among the stars
> calling
> for its own murder

Immediately Paterson identifies with the aging unicorn, as he returns to the scene of his first experience, ". . . to the old scenes." He visits the Cloisters and studies the tapestries that depict the unicorn's death and rebirth, and he declares for the first time the indivisibility of the virgin/whore who brings about the tragic consequences:

> The whore and the virgin, an identity:
> — through its disguises
>
> thrash about — but will not succeed in breaking free :
> an identity

The passages that follow describe literally what Paterson sees on the walls of the Cloisters, and his identity with the beast emerges in his admiration of the matchless beauty of the tapestry before him:

> The Unicorn
> has no match
>   or mate   .   the artist
>   has no peer   .

But Death too has no peer, and Williams intones the age-old elegy for life, which is evanescent, and for the imagination itself, which cannot be fathomed. But as he looks at the old tapestries, he reaffirms that art does survive. Art preserves, but so do man and woman — the innumerable women "each like a flower" captured by the artist. Williams' reference is to the hundreds of flowers in the tapestries, one of art's most beautiful and enduringly brilliant sights. His world, like that of the unicorn, has been dominated by the virgin and the whore with all her evocations — life and death, innocence and experience, purity and degradation, ideal and real — but she survives in the imagination of the artist who immortalizes her in art:

> — the virgin and the whore, which
> most endures? the world
> of the imagination most endures:

The advice that comes from the inner voice is to "WALK in the world," for to attempt to escape it into some unreal world of perfection, or to distance himself from reality (in the car or the plane), is to divorce himself from communion with it — to divorce himself from a world which is both virgin and whore.

Williams wrote to Viola Baxter as early as 1911:

> Virginity is a myth. A French youth tired of appetites went to his grandmother and said, "Grandma, when does passion end? Tell me because my soul would be free and virginal." She being very old answered, "I do not know." To be alive means you are committed against virginity either by yielding to passion or by holding passion off. It begins at the age of three and every blush proves there is no virginity.[31]

Paterson will walk in the world, seeing only the indivisibility of purity and corruption. To return to the "beginning" — the aim of all myth — is to know, (as his guide, the crone of "The Wanderer," instructed him) the secret world, like a snake "with its tail in/ its mouth." But he must first leap into the Passaic, the river of experience.

The next scene takes place in a whorehouse, and the prose passage is Gilbert Sorrentino's ribald account of his perambulations through first one

then another "Casa real"—until he is rescued by a friend who leads him to
a more "refined" brothel. There he sees "a smooth faced girl against a door,
all white . . . snow, the virgin, O bride . . . crook her finger and the vestal
not-color of it, the clean hair of her and the beauty of her body in the orchid
stench, in the vulgar assailing stench the fragility and you walk and sway
across the floor. . . . she is smooth-faced and wants four dollars." The
virgin/whore are an "identity"—a paradox of beauty and depravity. Sorrentino's depiction of the transcendent quality of this enigmatic "virgin" is close
to Williams' own sense of the oxymoron:

> . . . making love to a whore is funny but it is not funny as her
> blood beneath flesh, her fingers fragile touch yours in rhythm not
> funny but heat and passion bright and white, brighter-white than
> lights of the whorehouses, than the gin fizz white, white and deep as
> birth, deeper than death.

The experience with the virgin/whore is finally the experience of death
and life. It is Sorrentino's own sense of the indivisibility of those twin worlds
that touches a chord in Paterson and moves him to tell his tale of the unicorn
and the "virgin" who betrayed him. So Paterson returns to the tapestries and
describes the virgin who becomes the instrument of the tragedy. Like the
snake she carries the ". . . tail of her dress/ on her arm." Her ". . . brow is
serene/ to the sound of a huntsman's horn," the horn that will call the dogs
of destruction. He recounts the aura of death that envelops the innocent
beast—himself?—before he can be returned to life. Sankey believes that the
unicorn is a mythic embodiment, as well, of "Beautiful Thing"—his beauty
associated with the living beauty of the new country.[32] Paterson's song is one
of love nonetheless, for the unicorn loved the lady and yielded to her. "Loose
your love to flow," he tells the young, for rebirth lies in that communion.

The passage that follows is a love scene. The experience is a kind of
death as the lover loses all of his senses in passion, but he is "Peer of the
gods—," for as always in Williams' poetry intense passion, deathlike, holds
the promise of rebirth. In the midst of the poem, we are suddenly back in
the city of Paterson, as Paterson the man describes a woman on the street.
The portrait is close in spirit to many Williams drew in earlier poems. The
qualities are those of the strong survivor, his grandmother. She walks
rapidly, purposefully; she is neither short nor tall, young nor old. She would
appear to be a composite of all the women Williams admired: strong, slim,
imperious, free . . . and she wears a flower. She is the flower, and he vows
he will speak with her if he sees her again—this ". . . lonely and/ intelligent
woman." The ghost of his grandmother is evoked again in "It is all for you,"
as we remember the lines in "January Morning": "All this—/ was for you,
old woman./ I wanted to write a poem/ that you would understand."

In the next passage, dreams possess Paterson, who dances in
celebration—the old satyr; and in art, here the dance, "all the deformities

take wing." Williams enjoyed envisioning himself as the "satyr." The theme is strong in the earlier poem "Danse Russe" and others. In "Danse Russe," nakedness and beauty, the grotesque and the powerful, the ugliness and the goodness come together in the mythic figure of fertility and renewal. The magical quality of the ritual dance makes "all the deformities take wing."

The third section of Book V is devoted to Williams' much-admired model, Peter Brueghel. It is Brueghel who captured life as he saw it: "the unkempt straggling," but Paterson asks, " — how else to honor/ an old man, or a woman?" Brueghel ". . . saw it/ from the two sides . . . ," the world as virgin and whore, for the "imagination must be served —/ and he served/ dispassionately."

The final passage in the poem, and the end of the myth, comes with the recognition that "Paterson has grown older/ the dog of his thoughts/ has shrunk/ to no more than a 'passionate letter'/ to a woman . . ." But in the winter of his life, spring bursts forth. The rite of spring against the backdrop of Paterson's approaching death has the poignancy of Kore's own plight. Spring is life, and Williams evokes the Chaucerian spring in the flight of the birds, "moved by desire, passionately . . ." to new life. They go their separate ways, in pairs, "each to his appointed mating . . ." The marriage in nature is played out in the marriage season. He, himself, feels like the penned-up unicorn. It should be recalled that the symbolic interpretation of the unicorn myth in both Christian and secular versions implied marriage: in the religious sense a union with God, in the secular the marriage of the lovers. This is the "happy ending" of myth: the union of profane man with the sacred earth, connoting harmony, beauty, quiet. The *millefleurs* background of the tapestry depicting the Unicorn in captivity is equated by Paterson with that union:

> Now I come to the small flowers
> that cluster about the feet
> of my beloved

The theme of the tapestry's virgin and whore persists in his mind until he concludes:

> — every married man carries in his head
> the beloved and sacred image
> of a virgin
> whom he has whored   .
> but the living fiction
> a tapestry
> silk and wool shot with silver threads
> a milk-white one-horned beast
> I, Paterson, the King-self
> saw the lady

The poet continues his account of the story, protesting, "I cannot tell it all," yet recreating the luminousness, the beauty, the tragedy and the pain of betrayal, and the final union. He describes in full the virgin/whore and is obsessed by the expression on her face:

> — the virgin and the whore,
>   an identity,
>   both for sale
>   to the highest bidder!
>   and who bids higher
>   than a lover? . . .

He is ultimately ". . . a young man/ sharing the female's world/ in Hell's despight . . ." The passage closes with Emily Wellcome and the wrenching memory of her life that yet lives in the "old man." He tells the story of her betrayal by the soldier who left her with child to use her resources in the new world. Her voice is the last one Paterson hears: "The past is for those that lived in the past. Cessa!"

Paterson will sleep his life away, but not before he affirms the truth: "The measure intervenes, to measure is all we know,/ a choice among the measures. ./ the measured dance/ 'unless the scent of a rose/ startle us anew.'" I have noted elsewhere that for Williams the dance was the ultimate rite: dancing away our tragic deformities into the graceful, the Beautiful Thing. It is an act of survival against the insubstantiality of life and death. Dance is intrinsic to the motions of the river, the falls, the flow of time turning back ends to beginnings. Dance is the rite and play of primitive men and women who seek an integration lost to the modern, fragmented world. And, finally, dance is the *measure*, the rhythmic pattern of all art that encloses past and present into a permanent, enduring reality. At the end of *Paterson*, the poet returns to his own poetic beginning, in "The Wanderer":

> The (self) direction has been changed
>   the serpent
>
>   its tail in its mouth
> "the river has returned to its beginnings"
>   and backward
>   (and forward)
>   it tortures itself within me
>   until time has been washed finally under
>   and "I knew all (or enough)
>   it became me   .   "

Old but not without hope, Paterson's quest continues as he searches for those ephemeral moments when "the scent of the rose/ startle us anew." The poem does not end tragically; although the satyr dances "satyrically, the tragic foot," the poet dances, his art suggesting renewal, the rite of marriage. We recall Eliot's rite of spring in "East Coker":

> The association of man and woman
> In daunsinge, signifying matrimonie
> A dignified and commodious sacrament.

Book V of *Paterson* has witnessed several metamorphoses of the character of the hero, Paterson. They are, indeed, sea-changes that move step by step to rebirth. In old age he becomes the eagle on the crag; next, he takes on the attributes of the captured unicorn: "a horned beast among the trees." He becomes the dancing satyr and then the old poet tending his garden. Once more he is the unicorn against the *millefleurs* background (among the "flowers" suggesting woman and rebirth of spring); finally he is Paterson torturing himself in the filthy river that holds past, present, and future in its power. At the end, he is what he was in the beginning — Emily's grandson, sleeping his life away, recalling in dream the image of himself as dancing satyr, celebrating the scent of the rose, the renewal of life, the return to first things.

Book V[33] is a fitting close of Williams' myth: the virgin and the whore will continue to inhabit his world. Forever he will seek her; forever she will elude him. He will capture her in ephemeral moments of beauty beneath the tawdry veneer of his city. But in these moments she will bring him gifts: wisdom and experience and truth; a surge of life and a hint of death; the thrill of ideal purity and the passion of communion, drawing him to her inexorably in her mystery and complexity. As an old man, he knows from *experience* that "... love and the imagination/ are of a piece," that beauty and sordidness are indivisible in the modern world, and that Paterson, the man and the poet, will continue to search for the virgin and the whore and make of her an enduring Beautiful Thing.

Chapter VI
"Asphodel": Poems of Age

So let us love
    confident as is the light
        in its struggle with darkness

"Asphodel, That Greeny Flower"

Pictures from Brueghel is the book of William Carlos Williams' old age. Published in 1962, the year before Williams' death, the work is a mosaic of poems (many of which appeared earlier in magazines) that evoke the breadth and depth of a Brueghel painting. Its arrangement is spatial rather than linear, for Williams groups the sequences *(Pictures from Brueghel, The Desert Music and Other Poems,* and *Journey to Love)* to reveal the juxtapositions of the three worlds that formed his poetic experience.

In one way, the book is a tapestry itself—not unlike the French tapestries on the walls of the Cloisters. Here we find the *millefleurs* background ("... and a woman like a flower .../ Innumerable women each like a flower"): roses, chrysanthemums, violets, dandelions, irises, bougainvillaea, jasmine, eglantine, magenta, poppies, hyacinth, marigolds, daffodils, apple blossoms, hibiscus, and, finally, asphodel, "that greeny flower." The tapestry is a garden—flowers proliferating on every leaf—and in the center of it all is the broken unicorn, chained to the pomegranate tree in the winter of his life, enveloped by the season of spring. *Pictures from Brueghel* is Williams' final statement: it is his testament of faith in love, marriage, "no ideas but in things," the imagination, and art. Art, the poem, is his ultimate act of faith in his eroding world.

In some ways, *Pictures from Brueghel* is retrospective, reflective; more than that, it is a tribute to the regenerative spirit, "fastened to a dying animal," yet affirming the values held tenaciously over a lifetime.

Thus, *Pictures from Brueghel* is a work born of contentment after long struggle, a stasis of the spirit that implies not simply resignation by the aging poet, but the appreciation of a man who had written years before:

> For the beginning is assuredly
> the end—since we know nothing, pure
> and simple, beyond
> our own complexities.

Prophetically, Williams had written in *Paterson*, "never in this/ world will a man live well in his body/ save dying—and not know himself/ dying. . . ." But Williams knew himself dying, however slowly and painfully, and there is death as well as life on every page, as he sifts the experiences of past and present that nourished his imagination and that even gave new utterance to his thoughts.

As he had announced in "Writer's Prologue to a Play in Verse," "It isn't masculine more than it is/ feminine." So, too, in *Pictures from Brueghel*, his "matter" is of ". . . a woman and her lover, all/ mixed up, of life and death and all/ the secret language that runs through/ those curious transactions, seldom/ heard . . ." *Pictures from Brueghel* is both pictorial and aural; often the "voice," in its great range of tonality (lyrical, conversational, reflective, dreamy, cynical, imploring, nostalgic, assertive, and finally assenting), establishes theme as well as tone. He would even celebrate in "Asphodel" that the whole world had become his garden. He had learned that the world was both virgin and whore — that irrevocable truth first hinted by the spirit of the river in "The Wanderer," urging him to leap into the filthy Passaic.

At the end, in *Journey to Love,* Williams returns from his long wanderings to Flossie and to the abiding love and loyalty that now, in old age, he values highly. He had written as early as *Kora in Hell*, "The best that we have enjoyed of love together has come after the most thorough destruction or harvesting of that which has gone before." Now, much has gone before, and Williams reaffirms the female principle, the communion of love, and the "response of our deepest natures to one another."[1] Thus, in a particular way, *Journey to Love* is "Flossie's Book" — a book of last things.

Yet in a special sense, *Pictures from Brueghel* is a microcosm of *all* the themes and images that haunted Williams for fifty years. The careful reader can detect echoes from the Kore and unicorn myths, the journey through Paterson, the "real" world peopled by women he felt had "created" him (Emily Wellcome, Elena, Flossie), and the catalog of women — both virgins and whores.

He had written in "The Woodthrush," "fortunate man it is not too late," but the central theme against which all other motifs are imaged is human death in spring's season, and the book sets its atmosphere at the very beginning with the fall of Icarus. He wrote in *Paterson*, "Paterson has grown older," and the "aging body/ with the deformed great toe-nail/ makes itself known/ coming/ to search me out — ." The prophetic tone is reminiscent of Yeats' final poems, a kind of "summing up." Juxtaposed with death is life, and *Pictures from Brueghel* teems with portraits, glimpses, snapshots of Williams' favorite subjects: the young, virginal girls of Rutherford and of Brueghel's paintings who are the life surge that always revived him.

The theme of "woman" is therefore as significant in this final book as it was earlier, and the image of the virgin and the whore recurs in numerous poems in the guise of Helen or Venus or the worn-out dancer in Juarez, or in the covert references to the betrayed unicorn.

Among other patterns to which Williams returns is the journey of discovery, whether in *The Desert Music* or *Journey to Love,* in which the poet, like DeSoto before him, seeks out both the virgin and the whore, "an identity." The cycles of nature and the perennial theme of the death and resurrection of the land flow like an eternal river in *Pictures from Brueghel* and become a final source of faith and acceptance. A prevailing theme in this final volume is the figure of the poet-painter; the function of art and the artist is clearly an overriding preoccupation of a poet contemplating his own mortality. As in all Williams' poetry, the visible world is present in the female, without whom the imagination cannot "invent," and the conclusion that art transcends all is once more reiterated. We recall Paterson's question:

> — the virgin and the whore, which
> most endures? the world
> of the imagination most endures!

It is upon this world of the imagination that the curtain is raised in *Pictures from Brueghel*, and it is Brueghel's recreation of communal life that is most admired throughout the sequence.

The final large theme is, of course, Love, which closes the book. The tribute to Flossie is Williams' validation of his objective at the very beginning of his poetic life, best expressed in *Paterson*: "Rigor of beauty is the quest." The theme of Flossie is also the theme of the power of human love and marriage, communion and coherence, harmony and the renewal of life in the renewal of love in "that impossible springtime." Marriage, no longer prose, had finally become poetry.

Pictures from Brueghel

> "A
> world lost,
> a world unsuspected,
> beckons to new places"
>
> "The Descent"

In many ways, the sequence *Pictures from Brueghel* was the natural culmination of Williams' lifelong interest in painters and painting. As a child, he recalled Elena's paraphernalia of palettes and old tubes of oils lying around, long after her dreams of those earlier days as an artist in Paris had crumbled. Williams tells us both he and his brother Ed painted, and that art was one of his earliest passions.[2] At Penn, he met Charles Demuth, who remained a friend until Demuth's death in 1935, and during this early period he also met John Wilson, "a painter, a man in his early fifties ... whom I dearly loved."[3] He would spend days sitting around Wilson's studio, though he knew Wilson was "a failure of an artist" who "nevertheless had not lost the spark that made him love his vocation."

The "passion" never diminished, and years later, as he spent his days ferrying across the Hudson to French Hospital, he frequently stole off in the evenings to Greenwich Village to enjoy the heady company of the new

Bohemians. They were, indeed, an impressive and inspiring group: Man
Ray, Marcel Duchamp, Charles Sheeler, Marsden Hartley, and Walter
Arensberg. The walls of Arensberg's studio were glorified with the work of
Cézanne and Gleizes and Duchamp and others. James Guimond has ad-
mirably discussed the impact of the Precisionist school of American painters,
led by Sheeler and Demuth, on Williams' poetry.[4] During the 1920s,
Williams wrote that the principles of "impressionism, dadaism, surrealism
applied both to painting and the poem."[5] During his tour of Europe in 1924,
Williams visited many museums and talked with Sylvia Beach and Adrienne
Monnier about Brueghel.

   Years after, in a mood reminiscent of Yeats, Williams mourned the
passing of the world he knew and the artists now gone into oblivion, and he
eulogized the dead age:

> So here is Pound confined to a hospital for the insane in
> Washington.... Joyce dead; Gertrude Stein dead; Picasso doing
> ceramics; ... Brancusi too old to work; Juan Gris — at one time my
> favorite painter — long since dead; Charles Demuth dead; Marsden
> Hartley dead; Marcel Duchamp idling in a telephoneless Fourteenth
> St. garret in New York ...[6]

Williams' commitment to the painter and the art of the visual remained
an integral part of his poetry; his choice of the unicorn tapestries as an important image for his final book of *Paterson* testifies to the identification he felt
with other artists.

   One of Williams' earliest poems, "The Dance," is a tribute to Brueghel's
painting *The Kermess*. His admiration for an artist who could capture in permanent form the music, dance, and pageantry of the religious rite with
vivacity and realism was unbounded. The vitality which distinguishes
Brueghel's paintings, here in the lusty sensuality of the peasants, appealed
to Williams, who could perceive in the artlessness of the dancers the felt life
transformed to canvas. I have noted elsewhere[7] the importance of dance to
Williams as a vital human activity, so well reflected in Brueghel's paintings.
In this final volume, it is Brueghel's affirmation, indeed celebration, of a
meaningful inner life that Williams will juxtapose to the images of death and
disintegration that hover over him as he feels the slackening power of his own
body, yet still searching for renewal in the season of spring.

   The *Pictures from Brueghel* sequence begins with a poem whose title
is a bit ambiguous; is the "Self-Portrait" Brueghel or is it Williams? Or is it
a composite of the aging artist? Clearly the season sets the theme of the sequence; the time is winter, the painter "just the head and shoulders/ crowded
on the canvas," the nose bulbous, the eyes red-rimmed, the blond beard half-
trimmed; yet the artist is evident in the smiling eyes, the tilted, intent face
of one straining toward a canvas, the wrists delicate — a painter's hands, the
artist who has "no time for any-/ thing but his painting." Surely, it is

Brueghel, but the aging man, the intensity of the artist, the single-mindedness of the man also suggest the poet in the winter of his life, struggling against the pursuit of time. The strength of the head, the smiling eyes, red-rimmed, evoke the speaker himself. To crowd all on canvas has been his own intent.

Portrayed throughout the poems of the sequence are essentially four major motifs: the theme of death and decay, almost always in the season of nature's procreation; the theme of "woman" in all her innumerable sea-changes from childhood to age, virgin to whore; the theme of Flossie; and finally, returning to the symbol of Brueghel, the theme of the power of art over time.

"Landscape with the Fall of Icarus" touches upon the Greek myth of the tragedy of Icarus. As we know, according to Ovid and Appolodorus, Icarus, son of Daedalus, took flight from imprisonment wearing the fragile wings his father had fashioned for him. Heedless of his father's warning to keep a middle course over the sea and avoid closeness with the sun, the soaring boy exultantly flew too close to the burning sun, which melted his wings so that Icarus hurtled to the sea and death. The death of Icarus, the poet tells us "According to Brueghel," took place in spring when the year was emerging in all its pageantry. The irony of the death of Icarus, who has always been an emblem for the poet's upward flight that ends in tragedy, is that his death goes unnoticed in the spring—a mere splash in the sea. The fear of all poets—that their passing will go "quite unnoticed"—is an old and pervasive theme. That Williams reiterates the theme is significant in the life of a poet who always felt the world had never fully recognized his accomplishments. Now in old age, the fear recurs and becomes more dramatic in the image of the crucified stag in another poem, "The Hunters in the Snow." Again, as in "Self-Portrait," the season is winter, time of death and rebirth in Christianity. Here, in another Brueghel painting, the stag symbolizes Christ both in the inn yard at his birth and on the cross at his sacrifice. The harmonizing agents are the women, as Mary was the intercessor between man and God. Williams touches here on a favorite theme: The women tend the fire, signifying warmth and life, and reflect the vitality of the skaters, artists of a kind, patterning the hill. The presence of the painter, arranging the scene, is a key to the design of life and death in the painting. That Brueghel *completes* the picture emphasizes Williams' confidence in the artist to go beyond the experience of life and death to art, which surpasses both.

In another of Brueghel's paintings, "The Adoration of the Kings," birth is again celebrated in the winter season. The subject is the Nativity and the effect of the incredible event on the faces of the onlookers, but the key to the poem is Williams' appreciation of the "other" creator, the artist, who copied from the Italian masters their artistic virtuosity, their resourcefulness, the challenge to the painter that demands a work of art equal to the miracle of the Virgin birth itself. And the Italian masters rose to the challenge. Such is Brueghel's tribute. The vivid images of the "Babe in the Mother's arms," the "downcast eyes of the Virgin," transform the old story into something new and different. It is the downcast eyes of the Virgin that constitute the work of art in the poem and in the painting, so that the "miracle" emanates more from the shimmering Virgin than from the Christian birth. And it is the resourceful minds of the painter and the poet that subtly effect the change in emphasis.

In two companion poems, "The Woodthrush" and "To a Woodpecker," Williams plays on the now familiar theme of the aging poet. Winter is upon him, but "fortunate man it is not too late." The woodthrush, last voice of autumn, reaffirms the continuum that will lead to spring, but for the poet the thrush's message is silence ". . . without/ moving/ his dappled breast reflecting/ tragic winter/ thoughts . . ." We are reminded of Frost's Oven Bird (another term for the thrush), who also ushers in the season of dormancy in nature:

> The bird would cease and be as other birds
> but that he knows in singing not to sing.
> The question that lies framed in all but words
> Is what to make of a diminished thing.

The question that remains unanswered as the poet nurses his winter thoughts is whether it is, indeed, too late, and what can *he* make of a diminished thing?

In the second poem, Williams is more absolute for death: the December bird reminds him of death, a death often marked in primitive lamentation and anguished cries. The woodpecker is the nightingale of the winter, his song of mourning "harsh cry sounds" that clash with the deceptive backdrop of life: "woods hang out the snow as if/ it were gay/ curtains." But the "as if" — suggesting a condition contrary to fact — is only a reminder to the poet of the death in winter that mirrors his own finality. Williams' bare tree, the all-pervasive sense of the barren season, conveys faint echoes of Shakespeare's "bare ruin'd choirs, where late the sweet birds sang." Williams might well have been thinking: "In me thou seest the twilight of such day/ As after sunset fadeth in the west."

In "Song" Williams mourns the loss of sexual potency, so that, he confesses, he would rather read a book on the breeding of the heron than steal a glance at the fulsome woman passing by. Yet he goes on to declare:

> but I have forgot beauty
> that is no more than a sop
> when our time
>
> is spent and infirmities
> bring us to
> eat out of the same bowl!

The irony of the last line saves the poem from any sentimentality associated with the herons as he silently contrasts them with himself: "... the males/ in their mating splendor."

In "A Formal Design" the infirmities are again apparent in Williams' identification with the wounded, captive unicorn. The formal design is, of course, the poet's appreciation of the great beauty in art. The subject is tragic, for the magical beast is confined even though "lightly/ tethered." He is preserved, as it were, in eternal springtime in a tapestry "deftly woven," its "... milleflor/ design the fleur-de-lis." The pomegranate, Hades' tree of death, is the "fruiting tree" to which the unicorn is chained; and though death is never overtly mentioned, the broken beast, tethered to the tree of death, is an integral part of the "formal design" of permanent beauty in art. We know from *Paterson* that the poet identified himself with the captured unicorn, here preserved in the garden of life and death. The beast is held by a princely collar and his neck arches upward in a pose of aspiration and transcendence. Indirectly, the depiction recalls the betrayal of the unicorn by the lady, and the "milleflor" evokes the "innumerable women, each like a flower"—an eternal equation for Williams, even to "Asphodel, that greeny flower."

In a lighter vein, in "Exercise 2," Williams invites us to see him as he is in age: no more the romantic doctor stealing away to nightly trysts, but the friendly old man sitting in his garden greeting his neighbor across the hedge (see Chapter Four). Sexual "encounter" has come to mean smiling over the hedge at one's neighbor. So much for seduction in old age, Williams seems to be saying.

It has been my intention, throughout this study, to demonstrate that "woman" is a consistent theme in Williams' poetry from its earliest beginnings. That the image of woman took on varied and complex associations has already been revealed in the Kore poems, in the "innumerable women" of *Paterson*, and in a vast number of poems written over a fifty-year period. Now, in the winter of his life, Williams turns once again to the motif of the virgin and the whore and last thoughts on their evocative power in his poetic and prosaic life. But there is a difference, as one would expect from a man whose sexual potency had diminished and from a doctor who understands the gradual erosion of physical desire. The theme is more one of recollected passion and the tone one of realistic acceptance of life and the changes wrought as a man grows old.

Yet certain familiar themes recur and are affirmed as truths in Williams' lexicon. Innocence is forever an ideal, caught fleetingly in his world in ephemeral glimpses. Only the painting or the poem captures the evanescent moment of childhood. Conversely, the mystery, sensuality, and beauty of the whore is ever-present—the Venus that he no longer seeks but knows inhabits his world. "Love," the "he and she of it," is now translated into a less romantic and more stable foundation in marriage with Flossie as the chief source of fulfillment. But the idea of the virgin and the whore still haunts him and symbolizes the dichotomy of his polar worlds. He will declare finally what he had observed over a lifetime: "All women are not Helen,/ I know that,/ but have Helen in their hearts." Lastly, Williams clings to the female principle as the source of creativity in man, and this conviction, central to Williams' view of poetry, is central as well to his view of life.

In a group of three poems, "Peasant Wedding," "The Wedding Dance in the Open Air," and "Children's Games," Williams celebrates the rite of marriage, but more significantly offers a series of images of young, vivacious children and dancing women who symbolize purity, gaiety, and the life surge. "Peasant Wedding" depicts the enthroned virgin, the bride awaiting her bridegroom, and Williams' familiar touches merge with Brueghel's own vision of purity: the hair loose at the temples, the bride quiet and awkward, the isolation of virginity amid the clatter and chatter of the peasant wedding. For a moment, she is above the bustle of the scene — the reality of the world — but her remoteness will soon be dispelled by the expectant bridegroom. We recall Williams' observation in *Paterson*:

> — every married man carries in his head
> the beloved and sacred image
> of a virgin
> whom he has whored   .

In "The Wedding Dance" the bride seems not to be present at all. The scene is preempted by the lusty "ample-bottomed doxies" dancing riotously on the market square. The scene is earthy, as Brueghel's village housewives celebrate the female principle in the consummation of the marriage. The dance is a rite of spring, for the dance is performed in the open air and the gay rabble " . . . go openly/ toward the wood's/ edges." Interestingly, the poet emphasizes the power of the painter: the entire scene of activity and celebration is made permanent on Brueghel's canvas in all its lustiness and earthy gaiety.

In "Children's Games" the children are like the graceful tendrils of the new spring, young, vulnerable, beautiful, pure, and ingenuous. Though the boys swim "bare-ass," their innocence is even more touching; the girls are like flowers in motion or like children's pinwheels "to run in the wind with." There is freedom here, and the poet betrays a bit of envy for the small fry who can stand on their heads, roll a hoop, climb a tree in leaf, and disregard the knowledge and despair that awaits them when they grow up. This familiar theme, the evocation of childish innocence, needs to be set against the prevailing theme of *Pictures from Brueghel*, the fact of old age and declining power in a poet who would write in this period, "Sick as I am/ confused in the head/ I mean I have/ endured this April." The virginal life of young children, depicted by Brueghel and thus made enduring, must have served as a bulwark in the April he, the poet, struggles to endure, despite the reminders of approaching death.

Williams had written in a letter to Marianne Moore as early as 1935: "Heaven knows how much satisfaction Dante got from his hell which he writes of better than he did of Paradise."[8] Williams himself had no patience with Paradise, except as a fleeting dream. He saw around him, even in old age, too much of the hell of urban existence, too much of the betrayal of innocence and the erosion of native "purity." But equally important, he was suspicious of a hypocritical "purity" and had a healthy distaste for unreality. His letter to Marianne Moore continues:

> In too much refinement there lurks a sterility that wishes to pass too often for purity when it is anything but that. Coarseness for its own sake is inexcusable, but a Rabelaisian sanity requires that the rare and the fine be exhibited as coming like everything else from the dirt. There is no incompatibility between them.

Once, more, Williams had defined the inextricable nature of the virgin and the whore. Now in *Pictures from Brueghel* he again touches on the theme of innocence and experience, ideal and real, purity and sensuality as indivisible because "coming like everything else from the dirt." Even in a poem like "3 Stances"—three portraits of young women—there is a hint of the virgin and the whore. Elaine appears to be one the three Graces: an object of beauty, purity of motion, adventure. Her tentative smile is ingenuous, but she is aware of ". . . adult plans laid/ to trap her." The final picture of Elaine is the body poised like a bird in flight. But we are reminded of Williams' earlier wry observation, "The pure products of America go crazy," and we speculate on Elaine's "getaway." The second dancer, Erica, is almost a sculpture of perfection; yet to the admiring poet she is still a mystery, as all women are mysterious inward beings. Emily, the third dancer, is another vision of pure form and beauty and represents the woman Williams always loved: the proud head, the long legs, the promise and the genius of grace in motion.

But it is in the poem "Suzy" that the poet expands his theme of youthful innocence and potential power. In both "3 Stances" and "Suzy" the speaker is the poet-grandfather whose mixed emotions of pride, love, anxiety, and self-doubt affect his perception of the girls. Suzy is another Helen:

> women your age have decided
> wars and the beat
> of poems . . .

Suzy is a Koreate figure, victim and perpetrator: beautiful, tempting, like life itself, a flower, yet she will find hope and despair and, to the timorous old man admiring her, she offers a bunch of violets—an aroma of romance.

He yearns for her, but knows her to be unreachable. Suzy's power, her beauty and promising seductiveness are sources of anxiety and fear in the poet, who knows the ephemeral nature of innocence, momentary as the violets themselves, and the fate of that innocence in his modern world.

In "Song" Williams brings together several familiar motifs. The girl he addresses is Kore, "forever April," and though archly innocent, she hints at the theme of the whore, for the whore always knows more. The season is spring, but it is also invaded by the winter frost, a reference no doubt to the poet's own winter season. The merging of winter and spring in the embrace of the old man and the "blonde/ straight-/ legged girl" contain a touch of peril, as in attempting to recapture his own youth in her, he serves to diminish her youth and freshness.

In another "Song" Williams returns to the Venus theme: "beauty is a shell/ from the sea/ where she rules triumphant/ till love has had its way with her." The poem is a portrait of Venus' resurrection from the sea, and the poem seems a plaintive echo of the life force that haunted the poet to the very edge of death. The violation of Venus is also suggested briefly, for Venus is triumphant until raped by love—again the association of Venus with the virgin and the whore.

"The Title" is another return to the theme of lost virginity, here inspired by Gauguin's painting. Williams' poem is a recreation of the painting itself. The vulnerability of the woman, the need for protection, the images of fecundity and power combine to dignify the scene:

> the nude body, unattended save by a watchful
> hound, forepaw against the naked breast,
>
> there she lies on her back in an open field,
> limbs quietly assembled— ...

Williams' reverence for the nude body is reiterated in "Sonnet in Search of an Author": "Nude bodies like peeled logs/ sometimes give off a sweetest/ odor, man and woman/ under the trees in full excess/ matching the cushion of/ aromatic pine-drift fallen/ threaded with trailing woodbine." The almost sacred quality of the sexual union recalls the sleeping giants in *Paterson* in its primeval beauty. This idyllic vision is translated into communion in the modern world in "Some Simple Measures in the American Idiom and the Variable Foot": for a magical, breathless moment, there is contact between the aging man and the young woman in "The Cocktail Party." The poem is especially interesting for its unspoken assumption that this is all that is left for the old man—a fleeting moment of delight. The poem is a vignette of romantic attraction. Across a crowded room the poet meets a woman he has never known. Yet, looking into each other's eyes seems all that is needed.

> we looked in
> each other's eyes
> eyes alert to
>
> what we were saying

— and they find themselves "breathless" from this momentary encounter. For William Carlos Williams that magical communion—here in the eyes alone—was always an occasion of joy. He had once said, "After all there are only two kinds of us, men and women, the he and she of it,"[9] an awareness he never lost, despite age, infirmity, and loss of power.

He will finally pay tribute "To all the girls/ of all ages/ who walk up and down on/ the streets of this town," for they give order and beauty and design to an otherwise prosaic life. They "reform the line/ from here/ to China everywhere." It is always the woman who makes his existence intelligible and whom he will transform into permanent flowers in his poems.

In the end, it is to Flossie he turns, and in *Pictures from Brueghel* we meet Flossie through his many moods and recollections. There are snapshots of Flossie restoring life to the falling pink petal in "The Loving Dexterity"; Flossie showing him a "bunch of garden roses"—keeping fresh the beauty of the roses against the threat of decay; Flossie cleansing herself at her bath, no Venus, but a satisfaction and a joy; Flossie who could and would grant forgiveness for the wild years behind him. "The Stolen Peonies" contains, in a way, a double entendre as the poet "confesses":

> What I got out of women
> was difficult
> to assess

He reminds her what they have shared and lost, and he concludes that the loss of beauty brings husbands and wives closer than the happiness beauty initially brings. Williams will continue this theme in "The Ivy Crown" as he seeks to make his peace with the one woman who kept order, preserved life, cleansed everything around her through understanding and steadfastness. That he needed *all* women and that he needed Flossie too, that he needed their life force, seems to be a lifelong recognition in all his poetry.

The last poem in the sequence, "The Rewaking," is Williams' coming to terms with ends, and yet it speaks of another kind of revival. The poem is distinguished by its simplicity, its conversational tone, its acceptance of love as the answer when striving is over; it conveys the seriousness of Roethke's poem of final acceptance:

> I learned not to fear infinity,
> The far field, the windy cliffs of forever,
> The dying of time in the white light of tomorrow,
> . . . .

> A man faced with his own immensity
> Wakes all the waves, all their loose wandering fire.

Roethke's poem presents an image of death and life conjoined, and this, so it appears, is the essence of "The Rewaking":

> Sooner or later
> we must come to the end
> of striving
>
> to re-establish
> the image the image of
> the rose
> . . . .
> and so by
> your love the very sun
> itself is revived

Again, for Williams, spring is rebirth, and though he will accept the end of striving, Flossie urges him "not yet" to make his peace but to revive and reawaken in the power of love as nature takes new life and violets become lady's-slippers. But submerged in his bargain with Flossie is the surer knowledge that is also Roethke's: "He is the end of things, the final man." It is this knowledge he will protest in the first poem of *The Desert Music* sequence in *Pictures from Brueghel*. For here, as in earlier poems and signaled by "The Rewaking," is the theme of death and resurrection, birth and renewal, despair and a "new awakening."

The Desert Music and Other Poems

> Go home.Write.Compose   .
> Be reconciled, poet, with your
>
>   world, it is
>   the only truth!
>
> *Paterson II*

    The Desert Music and Other Poems is dated 1954, eight years after Williams had published the first book of *Paterson* and four years before the publication of Book V. He had decided to open the sequence with "The Descent," which appears in the third section of *Paterson I*, and his choice is revealing. The prevailing themes of *The Desert Music and Other Poems* are substantive to "The Descent" and, in a way, are fitting observations of an older man. The poem dramatizes a ritual already familiar to us in poems as early as "The Wanderer"—the cycle of death and rebirth expressed as descent and ascent. But the descent and ascent relate to more than the human cycle; they relate to the imaginative process itself. "The descent beckons/ as the ascent beckoned." Thus, the theme of creative initiation and renewal is

central to the poem, along with the motifs of the journey of discovery, love
in old age, and memory as a conduit for the rebirth of the imagination.
Memory is the option of old men; no longer active in life, they validate the
past as it regenerates in their minds:

> Memory is a kind
> of accomplishment,
> a sort of renewal

That Williams was conscious of his dead and dying world seems especially
moving in the entire volume *Pictures from Brueghel*, as I have noted; and in
"The Descent" there is a plaintive call for brave new worlds to be con-
quered.

> A
> world lost,
> a world unsuspected,
> beckons to new places

But the poet is always obsessed by what he has not accomplished, and so the
poem touches upon all that is lost in anticipation that leads him to descent.

By the time he comes to write *Journey to Love* the heroic call to action
will diminish. But here, in the closing years of his life, the poet, nevertheless,
reaffirms the lingering power of love. "With evening, love wakens/ though
its shadows/ which are alive by reason/ of the sun shining — / grow sleepy now
and drop away/ from desire." What we discover in *The Desert Music and
Other Poems* is a reawakening of hope and vitality and confidence, the
renewal of the mind, against all the facts of age and declining power. The
final stanza of "The Descent," which will lead to ascent, marks the whole
sequence:

> the descent
> made up of despairs
> and without accomplishment
> realizes a new awakening   :
> which is a reversal
> of despair.

The "endless and indestructible" descent is the necessary condition for the
"new awakening" which Williams will continue to reiterate in "The Desert Music," as he would in *Paterson*: "the river has returned to its beginnings."

In "To Daphne and Virginia" Williams brings together his already
familiar equation: woman, the mind, and the poem. He reaffirms his faith
in the imagination and its resourcefulness: ". . . We/ should be lost/ without
its wings to/ fly off upon." Again, the poem emphasizes renewal, shaping a

new world through the creative imagination, with woman as subject and object, to be snared by the mind and held by the poem. Here, Williams opens
up the world of women and his lifelong attachment to them:

>   . . . I,
>   who loves them,
>   loves all women . . .

In old age he rebels momentarily against the confinement of marriage as he
thinks of the world of women who have reached out to him:

>   And I am not
>   a young man,
>   My love encumbers me.
>   . . . .
>   There is, in the hard
>   give and take
>   of a man's life with
>   a woman
>   . . . .
>   something that wants to rise
>   and shake itself
>   free . . .

But the onetime lover knows, with touching realism, that age takes care of
such flights of freedom. His conclusion is wry and amusing at the same time:
". . . men/ against their reason/ speak of love, sometimes,/ when they are old.
It is/ all they can do   ." In old age, memory can only recreate in the mind
the passion of past experience.

Yet it is to become part of that woman's world he desires in his poem
"For Eleanor and Bill Monahan." More than any other poem in Williams'
corpus, the theme of the androgynous poet is clearly articulated. We recall
his early declaration: "I am Kora," but in this late poem, he not only
acknowledges again the female principle in art, but yearns to identify with
the Koreate springtime that is the procreant urge of nature's cycle. The poem
is one of the most beautiful expressions in modern poetry of the aspiration
for youth and rebirth in the face of death and disintegration. Fittingly, the
poem is addressed to the Virgin Mother, wellspring of all life, to whom he
submits himself. He dreams of "that impossible springtime/ when men/ shall
be the flowers/ spread at your feet." In the winter of the year, the wiser birds
have already escaped winter's blow; only man cannot escape suffering by
flying from pain. He confesses to being "half man and half/ woman" and
he addresses the "Mother of God" as both virgin and lover. In a few
brief autobiographical lines, the poet confesses his own pursuit of
love:

> There are men
> who as they live
> fling caution to the
> wind and women praise them
> and love them for it.

But now, in the season of age, he no longer pursues women but asks for a different gift. As an old man, he is satiated, but can still proclaim:

> The female principle of the world
> is my appeal
> in the extremity
> to which I have come.

The poem is most interesting for its honest appraisal of the years of pain, its submissive voice, its reassertion that man is not whole without the "female principle" which will empower him with new life "in the impossible springtime."

Serving as an appropriate prologue to *The Desert Music* is "The Yellow Flower," in which Williams reestablishes his earliest poetic dictum: "No ideas but in things." Once again, it is the motif of "The Wanderer"—that the poet's subject is life itself, however commonplace, distorted, obscure, or tortured. "The Yellow Flower" is important if only for Williams' statement that modern poetry takes its subject matter from reality, but it is also a harmony of beauty and ugliness, real and ideal, fact and imagination which distinguishes all great poetry for Williams. On a symbolic level, the yellow flower may well be a woman, the "crooked flower" which cures all men. Here the theme of the virgin and the whore is developed in all its complexity. If we examine the poem closely, the adjectives might easily describe the qualities of the virgin and the whore: the yellow flower is sacred, holds curative powers, survives in winter—an eternal flower with mysterious powers. At the same time, the flower is crooked, obscure, commonplace, "a mustard flower," ungainly, unnatural, twisted, strange, tortured, yet a flower that has picked him out "to hold me, openmouthed, . . . my will/ drained from me." Like Michelangelo, the poet chooses the commonplace yet sacred object as the subject of art. The poet's power, like Michelangelo's, is to see beauty in tawdriness, eternity in the sad, tortured lives of the artist's slaves or the poet's broken blossoms. In this poem more than in any other he would compose, Williams, at the end of his life, justifies his right as a poet:

> I have eyes
> that are made to see and if
> they see ruin for myself
> and all that I hold
> dear, they see

```
                also
                        through the eyes
                            and through the lips
                and tongue the power
                            to free myself
                                    and speak of it . . .
```

He is one with all artists who have chosen life — both virgin and whore — as the raw material for the creative imagination.

"The Desert Music"

> Human life is valuable "when it is
> completed by the imagination."
>
> "Spring and All" in Guimond, p. 30

"The Desert Music" is a micro-journey of discovery that reinforced forever Williams' notions about the relationship between reality and the world of art. As J. Hillis Miller has noted, "In 'The Desert Music' . . . Williams reaches the summit of his art." Miller bases this evaluation upon Williams' perfect reconciliation of the three elements existing almost precariously in his work: the formless ground (origin of all things); the formed thing (defined and limited); and a nameless presence (the "Beautiful Thing") that exists in every form but is hidden by it.[10] In other terms, the ground is the reality, the raw material Williams works with in his prosaic world; the form is the language with which he shapes its significance; and the Beautiful Thing is the work of art, that radiant gist he describes in *Paterson* as a fleeting moment of eternal beauty and truth. In many respects, the voyage into Juarez is the discovery of the chaotic common ground, the struggle to find the words to articulate its essence, and the recognition of the "radiant gist . . . always slipping away, fading, falling back into the ground, or being covered up."[11]

The poem begins with Williams' "drawing board" summary: "—the dance begins: to end about a form/ propped motionless — on the bridge/ between Juarez and El Paso — unrecognizable/ in the semi-dark." The passage over the bridge is an echo of Dante's voyage into hell; what the poet and his friends see are deformity, vice, vulgarity, chaos, darkness of the spirit. That the poem is a dance contains a special irony. The conditions of the artist's quest are conflicting; the dance and the motionless form posit the problem: "How shall we get said what must be said?/ Only the poem./ Only the counted poem, to an exact measure." The motionless form — that pitiful, debased shard of humanity — to be brought back to life by the dancing poet will become the "matter" of the poem. The scenes that unfold before him in Juarez seem to defy this lofty aim. He sees only misery, exploitation, crassness, and the obscenity of poverty, dirt, and disease. He has moved

from the fertile American landscape, from life, across the bridge to Mexico
and death. What he and Flossie experience is a debased culture mirrored
back in the paper flowers. The children begging, the general aura of
degradation, cheap tourist traps, and aching feet contrast sharply with the
almost virginal appearance of the young Indian girl and her baby, the three
half-grown children eating pomegranates, laughing, and lastly the old whore
in the cafe.

The portrait of the stripper is Williams at his best: earthy, humorous,
empathetic; like Toulouse–Lautrec, he knew well how to recreate the whores
of the modern world. Drawn to the stripper's vulgar sensuality, he enjoys her
show, but more importantly, he is touched:

> One is moved but not
> at the dull show . . .

The tone changes subtly, and gradually we sense that the whore is not
merely the worn-out trouper with the huge breasts; behind her is a screen
of pretty doves which "flutter their wings." She has the grace of a certain can-
dor, and though she is heavy on her feet, "That's good. . . ." He wonders why
he revels in the spectacle of the worn-out whore, and he finds the answer:

> The music!
> I like her. She fits
>
> the music   .

As so often in Williams' poems, he finds in the tawdry whore a kind of
knowledge she imparts to him: ". . . She/ at least knows she's/ part of another
tune." They leave the cafe, but the experience has been exciting for the poet.
For a fleeting moment, he has had a vision of the virgin and the whore in
the seedy cafe, and his heart exults. He is moved, changed, uplifted by the
experience of the "old whore" who can refresh him and ". . . raise to my ear/
so sweet a tune . . ." The remainder of the poem is an expansion of the mood
of creativity the experience has engendered. No longer do the words struggle
to come forth. The strains of the music echo after them, moving the poet to
hear the other music within — such music as Casals created with the cello,
profound and awe-inspiring.

Returning to the bridge, the poet sees the bundle of humanity gathered
in the angle of the bridge, and for the first time, he sees it is a man. Aghast,
he studies the human wreck reduced to the first emanations of life in the
womb: It is shapeless, armless, headless, "packed like the pit of a fruit," and
it wards its life ". . . against/ a birth of awful promise . . ." The music guards
it, and the scene takes on an almost mystical vision of death and rebirth as
the dance, the music, the poet's words usher in new life. Williams' final
revelation is sounded on a note of triumph:

I *am* a poet! I
am. I am. I am a poet, I reaffirmed . . .
. . . .
And I could not help thinking
of the wonders of the brain that
hears that music and of our
skill sometimes to record it.

The form of the poem complements his poetic quest: we begin and end
on the bridge. The fragments of conversation float up with the fragments of
peasant life. The sense of aimless wandering is transformed by the sense of
poetic mission at the end. Both the music and the dance are touched with
that aura of inviolable beauty, that rare moment of apotheosis in Williams'
poetry, when he is humbled by his own "skill sometimes" to raise the
Beautiful Thing from its secret hiding place, to record it in that eternal dance
he confirms in the poem. Williams had written in 1950, "[The poem] embraces
everything we are. . . . The poem . . . is the assertion that we are alive, as
ourselves — as much of the environment as it [the poem] can grasp."[12] It is here
that Williams might have said, as he did in *Paterson*, "Through this hole/ at
the bottom of the cavern/ of death, the imagination/ escapes intact. . . . You
can learn from poems." And his "education" in "The Desert Music" began
with the virgin and the whore.

Journey to Love

Journey to Love, the last sequence in *Pictures from Brueghel,* is dated
1955, eight years before William Carlos Williams' death, and the dedication
reads, "For My Wife." Indeed, *Journey to Love* is "Flossie's Book," and it
is more. In one sense, it is a book of final payments, a journey to death.
Williams made this journey over a very long period of his life, perhaps
because of his several crippling illnesses, perhaps because death was a
familiar friend he had known all his life as a doctor. If a writer lives long
enough, he feels himself moved to settle his accounts. Eliot, Yeats, and Frost
are only three examples of writers who composed "final" poems. *Journey to
Love* is such a sequence — Williams' thoughts on almost every subject that
had absorbed him over a long career as doctor and poet. The sequence is
reflective, often an inner landscape, though ostensibly addressed to Flossie
or the painters or "To a Man Dying on His Feet."

The themes are familiar to us as we move from poem to poem, hearing
Williams' voice — conversational, nostalgic, affirmative, contrite —
reiterating a lifetime's musings on love, marriage, death, survival, the
imagination, and finally "woman" in her infinite variety: the virgin and the
whore. He is still the unicorn in the field of flowers (thirteen different kinds
of flowers are named in *Journey*); his miraculous season is still springtime

with its beauty, fecundity, and unique "light" when ". . . the sun shines/ of a springtime/ afternoon." At the end of his life, he still evokes Kore's theme of renewal, and his equation of the female principle with the creative imagination giving meaning to the commonplace is his abiding truth:

the instant

. . . .

is all we have

unless — unless

things the imagination feeds upon,

the scent of the rose,

startle us anew.

Despite the modulations of the voice, the overall tone of *Journey to Love* is composed, accepting, assessing. Often, the voice of the poet is in remembrance of things past. Coaxingly, he reminds Flossie of the endless minutiae that gave moments of beauty to their lives. In this sense, *Journey to Love* differs from Williams' earlier work. Here there is no romantic abandon, no eroticism, no Don Quixote in a Model-T; no restlessness, rancor, complaint, or call to adventure. It is as though "The Desert Music" were the last journey *outward* bound. When we remember Eliot's trumpet call in *Four Quartets* ("Old men ought to be explorers . . ./ We cannot cease from exploration"), we find no similar imperative in Williams' final book. Nor do we approach the heroic stance of Tennyson's Ulysses:

Death closes all; but something ere the end,

Some work of noble note, may yet be done.

. . . .

Come, my friends,

'Tis not too late to seek a newer world.

Williams echoes Tennyson more precisely in Ulysses' later admission:

We are not now that strength which in old days

Moved earth and heaven, that which we are, we are . . .

Williams is the realist, less the Adamic man, and *Journey to Love* is more poignant because of his knowledge that the time for striving is past, though there is a proud assertion that the will has survived. Williams comes closer in spirit to Frost's last words in "Directive":

Here are your waters and your watering place

Drink and be whole again beyond confusion.

Williams had lost and found himself (*Paterson* bears witness to this experience); he reasons out his *Journey to Love* with wry humor and honest confession. He is whole again, beyond confusion, and he has captured in high lyrical fashion the commonplace transformed into the Beautiful Thing. Thus, *Journey to Love* is a "settlement" with himself, Flossie, love, art, life, and death.

An examination of individual poems in the sequence clearly demonstrates the scope and continuity of Williams' poetic experience. The overriding equation is the same we have met elsewhere in his work: woman, the imagination, and the poem. Woven into the very fabric of the sequence — not unlike the *millefleurs* of the tapestry — are images of women familiar to us by name: Kore and Helen, Flossie and Elena. There are the innumerable flowers of Paterson's streets, and the ever-present virgin/ whore. The emphasis in *Journey to Love,* however, is upon lasting things: marriage, love, art, and the language itself that preserves the experience to "startle us anew."

The first poem of the sequence, "A Negro Woman," is one of Williams' memorable snapshot portraits. The old woman is a black, middle-aged Kore, covered with marigolds, celebrating springtime. Though she waddles when she walks and though the delicate blossoms are wrapped in newspaper, she is ". . . an ambassador/ from another world." Notably she is bareheaded, an emblem in all Williams' portraits of freedom and ingenuousness, and she walks proudly in the early morning spring. Still in the urban wasteland, Williams can enjoy a whiff of spring and life and beauty in the figure of an ordinary woman.

The Kore theme is again touched upon in "View by Color Photography on a Commercial Calendar." The place he finds beauty is inauspicious as the title suggests, yet it produces a powerfully moving experience. The church, the apple blossoms evoking springtime, the peace of the surroundings of lake, mountain, and sky create an aura of calm and fulfillment. Spring is the season of promise, and the poem evokes not only hope but accomplishment

> by a calm lake
>   in the mountains
>   where the sun shines
>   of a springtime
>   afternoon. . . .

There is comfort here for a poet who also feels the weight upon him, as "something" is coming to an end for him as well but something "has been accomplished."

"The Sparrow" treats a subject not frequently touched upon in this last volume: recollected passion. "The Sparrow" is of course Williams himself — thinly disguised until the end, when he admits "This was I,/ a sparrow." The entire poem is about the mating season of the sparrow, who becomes both sexual pursuer and victim of the female of the species. At first he is all romance and passion, full of "manly" pride, fluttering his wings. In early spring, he loves. The generation of biological life is his contribution to the season of growth. An unlikely comparison is made between the sparrow and the unicorn—("... His image/ is familiar/ as that of the aristocratic/ unicorn ..."). The comparison seems absurd because the rare, cloistered unicorn is hardly as familiar as the common sparrow on the city streets. Yet for his size the sparrow is keen-eyed, truculent, and assured of his survival. His antics before the female are amusing and all too human; yet she is the cause of his death. Though he dies, forming a symmetrical pattern on the pavement "as if in flight"—an object of delicacy and beauty—"it is the poem/ of his existence/ that triumphed/ finally." The poem is interesting for Williams' statement that art triumphs finally over life, even in the period of biological creation. Death is the end for all sparrows, but the "poem/ of his existence" triumphs because it alone survives.

Probably the two most important poems in the sequence concern themselves with marriage, love, and, in "Asphodel, That Greeny Flower," the whole range of preoccupations Williams nurtured in these declining years. But the emphasis, even in "Asphodel," is upon Flossie and marriage.

"The Ivy Crown" is a very personal poem, realistic in its appraisal of love and marriage and human relationships. Fittingly, the poem begins with a reference to Antony and Cleopatra, also mature lovers who had been tested by time and events: "Antony and Cleopatra/ were right;/ they have shown/ the way. I love you/ or I did not live/ at all." Love in marriage is traced as a process, a dynamic of growth that must change or break "or find a deeper well." The poem touches upon a contrast between love for the very young, who are careless with it, and love for the older lovers, who nurture it, relinquish mere "romance," and accept a mature relationship that comprises both roses and thorns. The key to marriage, Williams tells Flossie, is the will to survive all of the onslaughts on love. Thus, the process of love is compared with the birth, growth, fruition, and death of the year; the need to survive the chilly season is accomplished by sheer will. Finally, the imagination saves love, making roses out of thorns. The poem concludes with a testament of faith from the pen of one who has grown older and presumably wiser:

> But we are older,
>   I to love
>   and you to be loved

It is easy, after the poet and his wife are dead, to either sentimentalize or excoriate the private lives of Williams and Flossie; to err in either direction is a breach of critical objectivity. Surely, the Williamses have suffered from both, especially in the recent vituperative attacks on Flossie Williams.[13] I prefer to rely upon Williams' own accounts until more dependable evidence is forthcoming. Whatever thorns enclosed the roses, the testimony at the end

of his life in both "The Ivy Crown" and "Asphodel, That Greeny Flower"
should be accepted at face value. Williams has made his peace with Flossie,
but more importantly he has demonstrated the power of their love in over-
coming "the sorry facts." The belief in the indestructible will is characteristic
of all of Williams' attitudes. That will is consistent, as demonstrated by the
very last lines of "Asphodel"—extremely relevant here:

> It is late
> but an odor
>   as from our wedding
>   has revived for me
> and begun again to penetrate
>   into all   crevices
>   of my world.

"Asphodel, That Greeny Flower" is Flossie's poem, but as I have suggested, Williams incorporated a wide variety of motifs that had recurred in
his poetry over fifty years. The poem is a song, and asphodel is clearly
Flossie, the common, everyday flower transformed through the imagination.
The asphodel has no odor, no distinguishing color—it is the color of common
grass, and wooden—but it is strong, survives, and takes him back to
childhood. Flossie had been beside him all his life, and the asphodel will symbolize "love, abiding love." "Asphodel" is a retrospective poem—it rambles
much as the mind of the reminiscing poet rambles, and the poem is a kind
of garden of beautiful flowers: buttercups, honeysuckle, lilies, apple blossoms, roses, daisies, violets, orchids, and all the flowers of their
childhood. But always the asphodel is present, sharing in the past, comforting in the present, celebrating the light of the future promised by the
imagination. Kore still haunts his thoughts: "I was cheered/ when I came first
to know/ that there were flowers also/ in hell." Now, with memory his only
link to the experiences of the past, the poet recreates childhood, the temptations of beauty in the world that beckoned to him (innumerable women, each
like a flower), their life together—less dramatic but more permanent. He
touches on the shared experiences; he seeks to make Flossie understand the
role of poetry in his life. It is the final gift he bestows upon her, the
poem.

> I come, my sweet,
>   to sing to you.

He reflects with some amusement that although he has not gone to hell for
her love—in the manner of Greek heroes—he nevertheless "found myself
there/ in your pursuit."

The subsequent sections of "Asphodel" are less personal and more
reflective of "approaching death," the function of art to defeat time that

threatens life, and love and art itself, which have fallen from grace. Williams inveighs against war and waste, the atomic bomb, the corruption of artists and art, even the drilling of oil. He returns to personal commitments and asks Flossie's forgiveness:

> In the name of love
> > I come proudly
> > > as to an equal
> > to be forgiven.

Her forgiveness renews him, and so he yields up the only gift he can offer her in return—the gift of the imagination, the poem: the "final flower." As always, Williams disarms us with the irony of this final humility, for his ultimate offering is always art!

"Asphodel" concludes with a coda that reaffirms Williams' belief in the triumvirate of love, the imagination, and the poem. Only through this union can we avoid destruction. The poem ends with confidence and triumph and a constant awareness of the darkness hovering over them in the final hours. There is a kind of quiet heroism to these final lines:

> Asphodel
> > has no odor
> > > save to the imagination
> > but it too
> > > celebrates the light.

"Asphodel, That Greeny Flower" is a celebration of a marriage that has transcended much difficulty, of a faith in the creative imagination that bravely confronts death and conquers it, of a poem that transforms the "sorry facts" into roses whose odor begins to penetrate "into all crevices" of Williams' world.

It would be unusual if Williams, even in a book of love such as this, would miss an opportunity to salute, finally, the virgin and the whore. *Journey to Love* is full of references to that paradox of innocence and experience, purity and knowledge, ideal and real that occupied his mind in all his poetry. "The King!" recalls Nell Gwynn, mistress of Charles II; Nell is a perfect union of good woman and erotic lover. Here we see her:

> She waked in the morning,
> > bathed in
> > > the King's bountiful
> > water
> > > which enveloped her
> > > > completely and,
> > magically,
> > > with the grit, took away
> > > > all her sins.

Charitable, kind, and graceful, she "served" the King's body, but in no way did that undermine her greatness. Williams concludes with the amusing observation:

> Happy the woman
> whose husband makes her
> the "King's whore."

In other poems, Helen and Venus and "love mounted naked on . . . a swan" (no doubt a reference to a painting of Leda, mother of Helen) make ghostly visitations. They are reminders that in old age Williams was still preoccupied with an image that circumscribed much of his world, both virgin and whore, and his experience, both real and imaginative.

Epilogue
Williams' Women
and the Imagination

"The only means [the artist] has to give value to life is
to recognize it with the imagination ..."

Imaginations, p. 115.

As a doctor, William Carlos Williams attended life; as a poet, he confronted death. By virtue of their profession, doctors commit themselves to preserve life: to set bones, administer drugs, usher in the birth of a baby, plumb the mysteries of the physical body—always fighting to keep the patient alive at all costs. Death for the doctor is often a personal defeat he does not accept with philosophical calm or equanimity. This was one side of Williams' life, and the miracle he brought away from it was the resiliency of life to renew itself—in the birth of a baby, in the creativity in women which he termed "the female principle." As a poet, he dwelled upon the biological limitations of man and the need for the imagination to break free from its confinement and, through language, to create something more enduring, more "enlivening"—capable of ensuring rebirth of the spirit and capable of outlasting the poet himself. Like woman, the artist was creative, and his poem, his painting, or his tapestry could transcend the "sorry fact" of biological limitations—to lift the world of the senses to the level of the imagination. He declared repeatedly over a very long life: "The world of the imagination most endures."

Because he was a doctor, because it was his experience to equate human birth with the creativity of art, Williams was able to bridge two worlds that on the surface seem irreconcilable. It is in this sense that we can appreciate his attitude toward women and his need to seek out the female principle in himself. His art was a product of the life surge within him, and Williams' "season" was always spring. He was not the first poet to seek to defeat time through art; such is the hallmark of every poet since the beginning of time itself.

In the poetry of Williams Carlos Williams the inspiration of women is at times romantic, at times erotic, at times enigmatic. He would not "preserve" romantic love so much as he would celebrate the fact of creation that all women symbolize, and, most crucially, unite himself with the female as a necessary act of "completion."

William Carlos Williams loved women. All of his poetry, prose, oral interviews, and experience proclaim that fact. "Love" is an all-encompassing word for Williams: it suggests esteem, admiration, desire, friendship, conflict, union, sometimes awe, and the recognition that woman is ever mysterious, contradictory, complex, and the source of life. Williams *liked* women and respected them as equals. His attachment to his independent

grandmother has been revealed in many poems; his identification with his
artist mother is moving and profound; his love for Flossie, for whom he may
not have gone to hell as he amusingly declares, was consistent and inspirational. Flossie herself is the subject of some of Williams' finest poems.
Whether in myth, in the figures of Kore and Demeter, or in the seducer of
the unicorn, he admitted an eternal fascination with women. They stirred
his imagination and brought his two worlds together. He lauded the poets
whose work he respected: Gertrude Stein, H.D., Denise Levertov, Kay
Boyle, Emily Dickinson, Marianne Moore. He admired the women who
stirred him to write poems because they had stirred his passions.

He writes of Matisse's great painting hanging in the Metropolitan
Museum of Art:

> Bare as was his mind of interest in anything save the fullness of
> his knowledge, into which her simple body entered as into the eye of
> the sun himself, so he painted her![1]

In reviewing Dr. Logan Clendening's book *The Human Body*, he ap-
plauded the author's courage for observing that "love is lovelier for its lust."[2]
He admired the virgin and the whore as the union of all that is innocent and
pure, erotic and mysterious in women. Commenting on the strippers in the
cheap dance halls, he writes:

> It is not the lusty bodies of the nearly naked girls in the shows
> about town, nor the blare of the popular tunes that make money for
> the manager. The girls can be procured rather more easily in other
> ways and the music is dirt cheap. It is that this meat is savored with
> a strangeness which never loses its fresh taste to generation after
> generation, either of dancers or those who watch. *It is beauty escaping,*
> *spinning up over the heads, blown out at the overtaxed vents by the electric fans.*[3]
> (Italics added.)

He had written in "Transitional":

> It is the woman in us
> That makes us write

And it was the women around him who served as catalysts for the creative
imagination—so much so, as we have seen, that Williams would come to
equate love, the imagination, and the poem as indivisible. In the coda to
"Asphodel, That Greeny Flower," he celebrates *finally* that union of love and
the imagination. It is his only answer to the despair and death all must endure, and it is a fitting coda to all his work:

> Only the imagination is real!
> I have declared it

                                      time without end.
If a man die
                  it is because death
                                          has first
possessed his imagination.
                            But if he refuse death —
                                    no greater evil
can befall him
                        unless it be the death of love
                                      meet him
in full career.
                    Then indeed
                                for him
the light has gone out.
But love and the imagination
                    are of a piece,
                                      swift as the light
to avoid destruction.

Notes

The following abbreviations have been used when citing the works of William Carlos Williams:

Auto.   *The Autobiography of William Carlos Williams*. New York: New
            Directions, 1948.
Imag.   *Imaginations*. New York: New Directions, 1970.
ITAG   *In the American Grain*. New York: New Directions, 1925.
IWTWAP   *I Wanted to Write a Poem*, New York: New Directions, 1958.
Kora   "Kora in Hell," in *Imaginations*.
Pat.   *Paterson*. New York: New Directions, 1946.
PFB   *Pictures from Brueghel and Other Poems*. New York: New Directions,
            1949.
Reader   *The William Carlos Williams Reader*. Ed. by M.L. Rosenthal. New
            York: New Directions, 1962.
SE   *Selected Essays of Williams Carlos Williams*. New York: New Direc-
            tions, 1954.
SL   *The Selected Letters of William Carlos Williams*. New York:
            McDowell, Obolensky, 1957.
Yes   *Yes, Mrs. Williams*. New York: McDowell, Obolensky, 1959.

Chapter I. "The Whore and the Virgin, an Identity"

1. "Asphodel, That Greeny Flower," *PFB*.
2. Paul Mariani, *William Carlos Williams: A New World Naked* (New York: McGraw-Hill, 1981), p. 695.
3. See "For Eleanor and Bill Monahan": "The female principle of the world/ is my appeal/ in the extremity/ to which I have come." *PFB*.
4. Richard A. Macksey, "A Certainty of Music, Williams' Changes," *William Carlos Williams: A Collection of Critical Essays*, ed. J. Hillis Miller (Englewood Cliffs NJ: Prentice-Hall, 1966), p. 139.
5. See Paul Mariani, "Paterson 5: The Whore/Virgin and the Wounded One-Horned Beast," *University of Denver Quarterly* 13, I, pp. 102–30.
6. *SE*, p. 196.
7. *Auto.*, p. 55.
8. *IWTWAP*, p. 16.
9. *Yes*, p. 3.
10. *Auto.*, p. 95.
11. *Auto.*, p. 224.
12. "On Women," *Interviews with William Carlos Williams*, ed. Linda Wagner (New York: New Directions, 1976), pp. 456–7.

13. "A Study of the Artist," *SE*, p. 213.

14. This and following excerpts from *SE*, pp. 196, 217.

15. *IWTWAP*, p. 64-5.

16. Leslie Fiedler, *Love and Death in the American Novel* (New York: Delta, 1966), pp. 320-324.

17. "On Women," p. 86-7.

18. Roy Harvey Pearce, "Williams and the 'New Mode,' " *William Carlos Williams*, ed. Miller, p. 104.

19. Edith Hamilton, *Mythology* (New York: Little, Brown, 1940), p. 34.

20. Homer W. Smith, *Man and His Gods* (New York: Grosset & Dunlap, 1952), p. 126.

21. Robert Graves, *The Greek Myths*, vol. 2 (Baltimore: Penguin, 1955), p. 212.

22. Nikos Kazantzakis, *Report to Greco* (New York: Simon & Schuster, 1945), p. 149.

23. John H. Emminghaus, *Mary Magdalene, The Saints in Legend and Art*, (West Germany: V.A.B. Recklinhausen), pp. 5-8.

24. James Joyce, "Araby," *Dubliners* (New York: Viking, 1916). This and following excerpts pp. 31, 35.

25. Hugh Kenner, "*The Portrait* in Perspective," *James Joyce, A Portrait of the Artist as a Young Man: Text, Criticism & Notes*, ed. Chester Anderson (New York: Viking, 1968), p. 436.

26. F. Scott Fitzgerald, *The Great Gatsby* (New York: Scribner's, 1925), p. 148.

27. *Auto.*, p. 3.

28. T.S. Eliot, "The Metaphysical Poets," *Selected Essays* (New York: Harcourt, Brace, & World, 1932), p. 243.

29. "On Women," p. 66.

30. Interview with Walter Sutton, *Interviews*, ed. Wagner, p. 54.

31. Sutton, p. 54.

32. Brendan Gill in a *New Yorker* profile, quoted by Reed Whittemore, *William Carlos Williams: Poet from Jersey* (New York: Houghton Mifflin, 1975), p. 305.

33. *Kora*, p. 61.

34. *Auto.*, pp. 81 and ff.

35. *Kora*, p. 42.

36. *Auto.*, p. 222.

37. Mariani, p. 107.

Chapter II. "Spring and All": The Myth of Demeter/Kore

1. *SE*, p. 196.

2. Carl Jung and C. Kerenyi, *Essays on a Science of Mythology*, Bollingen Series XXII (Princeton, NJ: Princeton University, 1941), p. 48.

3. Jung, p. 188.

4. Jung, p. 177.

5. *Auto.*, p. 146.

6. Audrey T. Rodgers, "William Carlos Williams's 'New World': Images of the Dance," *Arizona Quarterly* 35 (Spring 1979).

7. Lillian Feder, *Ancient Myth in Modern Poetry* (Princeton NJ: Princeton University, 1971), p. 33.

8. *Imag.*, pp. 3-4.

9. *Imag.*, pp. 3-4.

10. Feder, pp. 200 ff.

11. *Imag.*, p. 29.

12. David Bidney, "Myth, Symbolism, and Truth," *Myth, a Symposium*, ed. Thomas A. Sebeok (Bloomington IN: Indiana University, 1955), p. 20.

13. F. Nietzsche, *The Birth of Tragedy*, ed. F. Golffing (New York: Anchor, 1956), p. 36-7.

14. Richard Chase, *Quest for Myth* (Baton Rouge LA: Louisiana State University, 1949), p. 15.

15. *IWTWAP*, p. 80.

16. "Spring and All," *Imag.*, p. 116.

17. *Interviews*, Wagner, p. 76.

18. Sir James Frazer, *The New Golden Bough* (New York: Mentor, 1959), pp. 423-38.

19. Robert Graves, *The Greek Myths*, Vol. I (Baltimore: Penguin, 1955), p. 91.

20. Graves, p. 92.

21. Feder, p. 207.

22. Phyllis Chesler, *Women and Madness* (New York: Avon, 1972), p. xiv.

23. Jung and Kerenyi, *Essays*, p. 12.

24. Jung and Kerenyi, *Essays*, p. 128.

25. Jung, this and ff. in *Essays*, pp. 157-73.

26. Pearce, p. 104.

27. *Auto.*, p. 60-1.

28. Whittemore, p. 295.

29. Bernetta Quinn, "On *Paterson, Book I*," *William Carlos Williams*, ed. Miller, p. 117.

30. Kazantzakis, p. 149.

31. Whittemore, p. 199.

32. This and ff. in *ITAG*, p. 45.

33. D.H. Lawrence, *Phoenix* (New York: Viking, 1936), p. 335.

34. Whittemore, p. 200.

35. *ITAG*, p. 236.

36. Mariani, p. 633.

37. *SL*, p. 305.

38. Carl Jung, "Aion: Phenomenology of the Self," *The Portable Jung*, ed. Joseph Campbell (New York: Penguin, 1971), 139-162.

39. Jung, "Aion," p. 150.

40. Mariani, p. 486, 594.

41. *Auto.*, p. 55.

42. *IWTWAP*, p. 26.

43. James Guimond, *The Art of William Carlos Williams* (Urbana IL: University of Illinois, 1966), p. 25ff.

44. *Auto.*, p. 158.

45. *IWTWAP*, p. 14.

46. *Kora*, p. 60.

Chapter III. From Myth to Reality: The "Innumerable Women"

1. Macksey, p. 137.

2. Macksey, p. 137.

3. *IWTWAP*, p. 26.

4. *Auto.*, p. 91.

5. *Auto.*, p. 4.

6. *IWTWAP*, p. 1.

7. Whittemore, pp. 137ff.

8. Whittemore, pp. 13ff.

9. Mariani, p. 5.

10. *Auto.*, p. 108.

11. Whittemore, p. 86.

12. *Auto.*, p. 167–8.

13. *Interviews*, ed. Wagner, p. 76, 93.

14. *Yes*, p. 94.

15. Letter to Flossie, September 28, 1927, *SL*.

16. Whittemore, p. 16.

17. *Yes*, p. 5.

18. Letter to Helen Russell, Oct. 22, 1949, *SL*.

19. Whittemore, p. 23.

20. *Kora*, p. 8.

21. *IWTWAP*, p. 1.

22. Whittemore, p. 28.

23. Whittemore, p. 40.

24. *Kora*, p. 63.

25. *Yes*, p. 130.

26. *Yes*, p. 141–2.

27. Letter to Marianne Moore, October 18, 1935, *SL*.

28. *Interviews*, ed. Wagner, p. 77.

29. Letter to W. Andrews, March 1, 1932, *SL*.

30. Rod Townley, *The Early Poetry of William Carlos Williams* (Ithaca NY: Cornell University, 1975), p. 65.

31. *Yes*, p. 109.

32. *Kora*, p. 62.

33. *Kora*, p. 94.

34. *Yes*, p. 24.

35. *Yes*, p. 27–8.

36. *Yes*, p. 31.

37. Mariani, p. 79.

38. Whittemore, p. 72.

39. Whittemore, p. 198.

40. Whittemore, p. 198.

41. Letter to Flossie, 1927, *SL*.

42. *Kora*, p. 22.

43. Whittemore, p. 147.

44. Mariani, p. 504.

45. Letter to Marianne Moore, 1921, *SL*.

46. William Pritchard, *Lives of the Modern Poets* (New York: Oxford University Press, 1980), p. 278.

47. Letter to Robert McAlmon, May 25, 1939, *SL*.

48. Letter to James Laughlin, 1946 (Beineke Library Collection, Yale University).

49. Whittemore, p. 341.

50. Letter to James Laughlin, July 5, 1945 (Beineke Library Collection, Yale University).

51. *Interviews*, ed. Wagner, p. 175.

52. Townley, p. 130.

53. Townley, p. 175.

54. Letter to Edgar I. Williams, April 12, 1905, *SL*.

55. *IWTWAP*, p. 7.

56. *Reader*, p. 391.

57. *Kora*, p. 10.

58. *Interviews*, ed. Wagner, p. 40.

59. Letter to Viola Baxter, 1910, *SL*.

60. Mariani, p. 58.

61. Letter to Viola Baxter, Dec. 1, 1911 (Beineke Library Collection, Yale University).

62. Whittemore, p. 154.

63. Joseph Riddel, *The Inverted Bell: Modernism and the Counterpoetics of William Carlos Williams* (Baton Rouge LA: Louisiana State University, 1974), p. 4.

64. *Auto.*, pp. 166ff.

65. *Auto.*, p. 169.

66. William Carlos Williams, "The Baroness Elsa Von Freitag Loringhoven," (This and following from Beineke Library Collection, Yale University).

67. Whittemore, p. 228.

68. Letter to James Laughlin, Feb. 14, 1939 (Beineke Library Collection, Yale University).

Chapter IV. The Emerging Image: Women in Williams' Shorter Poems, 1910–1950

1. *Auto.*, p. 46.

2. *Auto.*, p. 47.

3. Guimond, p. 12.

4. William Carlos Williams, "A Matisse," *A Novelette and Other Prose, Contact, II* (1921), pp. 20-1.

5. *ITAG*, p. 59.

6. Townley, p. 81.

7. *Interviews*, ed. Wagner, p. 76.

8. Ezra Pound, *The Literary Essays of Ezra Pound*, ed. T.S. Eliot (New York: New Directions, and London: Faber and Faber, 1954), p. 4.

9. Hugh Kenner, *The Pound Era* (Berkeley CA: University of California Press, 1971), pp. 182–5.

10. *Kora*, p. 15.

11. "Foreword," *Auto*.

12. *Kora*, p. 4.

13. Mike Weaver, *William Carlos Williams, The American Background* (Cambridge: Cambridge University Press, 1971), p. 28.

14. Letter to Kenneth Burke, August 14, 1943 (Pennsylvania State University Collection).

15. *Kora*, p. 19.

Chapter V. *Paterson*: "Beautiful Thing"

1. See p. 2-3.

2. See "Author's Note," *Pat*.

3. *SE*, p. 196.

4. Guimond, p. 221.

5. Mariani, p. 697.

6. Letter to Viola Baxter, 1911. (Beineke Library Collection, Yale University).

7. See Feder, p. 54.

8. Ernst Cassirer, *The Philosophy of Symbolic Forms*, Vol. 2, *Mythical Thought*, (New Haven CT: Yale University, 1955), p. 218.

9. Whittemore, p. 281.

10. Williams had commented to Hugh Kenner in 1957, "You need a poet, otherwise it would all die voiceless." In *The Pound Era*, p. 512.

11. Benjamin Sankey, *A Companion to William Carlos William's* Paterson, (Berkeley CA: University of California Press, 1971), p. 12.

12. Mariani, pp. 461 ff.

13. Letter to Viola Baxter, 1911 (Beineke Library Collection, Yale University).

14. Mariani, p. 543.

15. Mariani, p. 415.

16. Letter to Viola Baxter, 1911 (Beineke Library Collection, Yale University).

17. Guimond, p. 193.

18. Quoted by John Thirlwall from dust jacket, *Pat. III*, in Thirlwall, "William Carlos Williams' Paterson: The Search for the Redeeming Language—A Personal Epic in Five Parts," New Directions, 17, 1961.

19. Thirlwall, p. 256.

20. Pearce, p. 104.

21. Guimond, p. 203ff.

22. Margaret B. Freeman, *The Unicorn Tapestries* (The Metropolitan Museum of Art, New York: Dutton, 1976). The following account derives from Freeman's analysis.

23. The following is Odell Shephard's translation of Ludwig Uhland's poem, in Freeman, p. 11:

> I stood in the Maytime meadows
>   by roses circled round
> Where many a fragile blossom
>   Was bright upon the ground;
> And as though the roses called them
>   And their wild hearts understood,
> The little birds were singing
>   In the shadows of the wood.
> The nightingale among them
>   Sang sweet and loud and long,
> Until a greater voice than hers
>   Rang out above her song.
> For suddenly between the crags,
>   Along a narrow vale
> The echoes of a hunting horn
>   Came clear along the gale.
> The hunter stood beside me
>   Who blew the mighty horn,
> I saw that he was hunting
>   The noble unicorn....
> The unicorn is noble;
>   He keeps him safe and high
> Upon the narrow path and steep
>   Climbing to the sky;

> And there's no man can take him;
>   He scorns the hunter's dart
> And only a virgin's magic power
>   Shall tame his haughty heart.
> What would be now the state of us
>   But for this unicorn,
> And what would be the fate of us,
>   Poor sinners, lost, forlorn?
> Oh may He lead us on and up,
>   Unworthy though we be,
> Into His Father's kingdom
>   To dwell eternally.

24. Linda Sipress, Adaptation of Margaret Freeman, *The Unicorn Tapestries*, (Metropolitan Museum of Art, 1974), "Fragments from the Fifth Tapestry."

25. Freeman, p. 318.

26. Mariani, p. 106-7.

27. Letter to James Laughlin, Sept. 9, 1949 (Beineke Library Collection, Yale University).

28. Guimond, p. 203.

29. J. Hillis Miller, *Poets of Reality* (New York: Atheneum, 1969), p. 295.

30. Miller, pp. 322-6.

31. Letter to Viola Baxter, 1911 (Beineke Library Collection, Yale University).

32. Sankey, p. 215.

33. Williams began a sixth book of *Paterson* in 1961, but never completed more than four pages; the fragments were found after his death. Interestingly, the same themes still possessed him. The fragments present images of the ever-present falls, the haunting events of the past, the objects of beauty surprisingly discovered among the prosaic, and the figure of a betrayed woman, "Lucy" whose "father sold her/ to Charlie." The loveliest lines were written by the old, paralyzed poet on January 8, 1961:

> Dance, dance! loosen your limbs from that art which holds you
> faster than the drugs which hold you faster — dandelion on
> my bedroom wall.

Chapter VI. "Asphodel": Poems of Age

1. Letter to Flossie, Sept. 8, 1927, in *Kora*, p. 22.

2. *Auto.*, p. 47.

3. *Auto.*, this and following on p. 61.

4. Guimond, pp. 41–62.

5. *Auto.*, p. 148.

6. *Auto.*, p. 318.

7. Audrey T. Rodgers, *The Universal Drum: Dance Imagery in the Poetry of Eliot, Crane, Roethke and Williams* (University Park: Pennsylvania State University, 1979), pp. 139ff.

8. This and following in letter to Marianne Moore, Oct. 18, 1935, *SL*, p. 186.

9. *IWTWAP*, p. 65.

10. Miller, pp. 328ff.

11. Miller, p. 336.

12. *SL*, p. 286.

13. Ellen Reiss, "Who Hurt W.C. Williams?" *The Right to Aesthetic Realism to Be Known* 44 (Sept. 16, 1981), Aesthetic Realism Foundation, Inc.

Epilogue: Williams' Women and the Imagination

1. "A Matisse," *Imag.*, p. 321.
2. *Imag.*, p. 363.
3. *Kora*, p. 75–6.

Primary Sources
(from the Works
of William Carlos Williams)

The Autobiography of William Carlos Williams. New York: New Directions, 1948.
The Collected Earlier Poems of William Carlos Williams. New York: New Directions, 1966.
The Collected Later Poems of William Carlos Williams. New York: New Directions, 1966.
I Wanted to Write a Poem: The Autobiography of a Poet. New York: New Directions, 1958.
Imaginations. New York: New Directions, 1970.
In the American Grain. New York: New Directions, 1925.
"Kora in Hell," in *Imaginations.*
Paterson. New York: New Directions, 1946.
Pictures from Brueghel and Other Poems. New York: New Directions, 1949.
Selected Essays of William Carlos Williams. New York: New Directions, 1954.
The Selected Letters of William Carlos Williams. New York: McDowell, Obolensky, 1957.
The William Carlos Williams Reader. Ed. by M.L. Rosenthal. New York: New Directions, 1962.
Yes, Mrs. Williams. New York: McDowell, Obolensky, 1959.
Unpublished Work:
Letters to James Laughlin, Beineke Library Collection, Yale University.
Letters to Viola Baxter, Beineke Library Collection, Yale University.
Letter to Kenneth Burke, Pattee Library Collection, The Pennsylvania State University.
"The Baroness Elsa Von Freitag Loringhoven," Beineke Library Collection, Yale University.

Bibliography

Bidney, David. "Myth, Symbolism, and Truth." In *Myth, a Symposium*, ed. by Thomas A. Sebeok. Bloomington IN: Indiana University Press, 1955.

Brinnin, John. *William Carlos Williams*. University of Minnesota Pamphlets, no. 24. Minneapolis MN: University of Minnesota Press, 1963.

Cassirer, Ernst. *The Philosophy of Symbolic Forms*, Vol. 2, *Mythical Thought*. New Haven CT: Yale University Press, 1955.

Chase, Richard. *Quest for Myth*. Baton Rouge LA: Louisiana State University Press, 1949.

Chesler, Phyllis. *Women and Madness*. New York: Avon, 1972.

Coles, Robert. "William Carlos Williams, a Writing Physician," *The Journal of the American Medical Association* 245, 1, Jan. 2, 1981.

_____. *William Carlos Williams: The Knack of Survival in America*. New Brunswick NJ: Rutgers University Press, 1975.

De Witt, John Francis. *The Beautiful Thing: William Carlos Williams and Women*. Ph.D. dissertation (DA 2618A), University of Connecticut, 1973.

Eliot, T.S. *Selected Essays*. New York: Harcourt, Brace, & World, 1950.

Feder, Lillian. *Ancient Myth in Modern Poetry*. Princeton NJ: Princeton University Press, 1971.

Frazer, Sir James. *The New Golden Bough*. New York: Mentor, 1959.

Freeman, Margaret B. *The Unicorn Tapestries*. The Metropolitan Museum of Art, New York: E.P. Dutton, 1976.

Graves, Robert. *The Greek Myths*. Baltimore: Penguin, 1955.

_____. *The White Goddess*. New York: Farrar, Straus, & Giroux, 1966.

Guimond, James. *The Art of William Carlos Williams*. Urbana IL: University of Illinois Press, 1966.

Hamilton, Edith. *Mythology*. New York: Little, Brown, 1940.

Heyen, William. "The Poet's Leap into Reality." In *Profile of William Carlos Williams*, ed. by Jerome Mazzaro. Columbus OH: Charles E. Merrill, 1971.

Jung, Carl. "The Poet." In *The Norton Reader*, ed. by Arthur M. Eastman. New York: Norton, 1980.

_____, and Kerenyi, C. *Essays on a Science of Mythology*. Bollingen Series XXII. Princeton NJ: Princeton University Press, 1949.

Joyce, James. *Dubliners*. New York: Viking, 1916.

Kazantzakis, Nikos. *Report to Greco*. New York: Simon & Schuster, 1945.

Kenner, Hugh. *The Pound Era*. Berkeley: University of California Press, 1971.

Koch, Vivienne. *William Carlos Williams*. Norfolk VA: New Directions, 1950.

Macksey, Richard A. "A Certainty of Music: Williams' Changes." In *William Carlos Williams: A Collection of Critical Essays*, ed. by J. Hillis Miller. Englewood Cliffs NJ: Prentice-Hall, 1966.

Mariani, Paul. "*Paterson V:* The Whore/Virgin and the Wounded One-Horned Beast," *University of Denver Quarterly*, 13, I. Denver CO: University of Denver Press.

_____. *William Carlos Williams: A New World Naked*. New York: McGraw Hill, 1981.

Mazzaro, Jerome, ed. *Profile of William Carlos Williams*. Columbus OH: Chas. E. Merrill, 1971.

Miller, J. Hillis. *Poets of Reality: Six Twentieth-Century Writers*. New York: Atheneum, 1969.

_____, ed. *William Carlos Williams: A Collection of Critical Essays*. Englewood Cliffs NJ: Prentice Hall, 1966.

Nietzsche, F. *The Birth of Tragedy*, ed. by F. Golffing. New York: Anchor, 1956.

Pearce, Roy Harvey. *The Continuity of American Poetry*. Princeton NJ: Princeton University Press, 1961.

Pound, Ezra. *The Literary Essays of Ezra Pound*. New York: New Directions, 1935.

Pritchard, William H. *Lives of the Modern Poets*. New York: Oxford University Press, 1980.

Quinn, Sister Bernetta M. *The Metamorphic Tradition in Modern Poetry*. New York: Gordian, 1966.

Reiss, Ellen. "Who Hurt W.C. Williams?" *The Right of Aesthetic Realism to Be Known* 44 (Sept. 16, 1981). Aesthetic Realism Foundation, Inc.

Rexroth, Kenneth. *American Poetry in the 20th Century*. New York: Seabury, 1973.

Riddel, Joseph N. *The Inverted Bell: Modernism and the Counterpoetics of William Carlos Williams*. Baton Rouge LA: Louisiana State University Press, 1974.

Rodgers, Audrey T. *The Universal Drum: Dance Imagery in Eliot, Crane, Roethke and Williams*. University Park PA: Pennsylvania State University Press, 1979.

_____. "William Carlos Williams's 'New World': Images of the Dance." *Arizona Quarterly* (Spring 1979), Spring, 35, 1.

Rosenthal, M.L. *The Modern Poets*. London: Oxford University Press, 1960.

Sankey, Benjamin. *A Companion to William Carlos Williams's* Paterson. Berkeley CA: University of California Press, 1971.

Sipress, Linda. Adaptation of Margaret Freeman, *The Unicorn Tapestries*. New York: Metropolitan Museum of Art, 1974.

Smith, Homer. *Man and His Gods*. New York: Grosset & Dunlap, 1952.

Townley, Rod. *The Early Poetry of William Carlos Williams*. Ithaca NY: Cornell University Press, 1972.

Wagner, Linda W., ed. *Interviews with William Carlos Williams*, transcribed by John Thirlwall. New York: New Directions, 1976.

Weaver, Mike. *William Carlos Williams: The American Background*. Cambridge: Cambridge University Press, 1971.

Weiss, Jeri Lynn. *The Feminine Assertion: Women in the World of William Carlos Williams*. Ph.D. dissertation (DA 344A), University of California, 1973.

Whitaker, Thomas R. *William Carlos Williams*. New York: Twayne, 1968.

Whittemore, Reed. *William Carlos Williams: Poet from Jersey*. Boston: Houghton Mifflin, 1975.

Woods, Powell. "William Carlos Williams: The Poet as Engineer." In *Profile of William Carlos Williams*, ed. by Jerome Mazzaro. Columbus OH: Charles E. Merrill, 1971.

Index